crazy LIFE

Praise for
crazy LIFE

"The chapters I read in your book opened my heart and stirred my spirit. I have been keeping so much pain inside since the death of my nephew and his father that I related to your journey. I navigated through the questions at the end of the chapters and found so much peace. I cannot wait to get the whole book in print so I can utilize it as a tool for the 7,000 women in my National Area, and also for my personal studies with my extended spiritual family."

—**Jan Harris**, (Retired) Former #1 National
Sales Director/Pearl, Mary Kay, Inc.

"While flying to Oakland today we had a four-hour delay in Boise. I decided to read through the two chapters you sent. Wow. Maybe I'm loving it because we have the same approach and style, but this is really good stuff! Opening your life and heart certainly draws people to you. I love it and would be honored to support this project…"

—**Dr. Jim Grassi**, Founder,
Men's Ministry Catalyst and Author

"Dr. Tony Nelson is an enigma. Refreshingly honest, he's a scholar from the working class; no less a stranger to agony than he is to beauty and riches. Tony is a manly man who loves outdoor adventure and hard work; yet, he is an artist and a healer who believes in the power of women. He knows how to celebrate and adores his family. For thirty years, Tony has led by tending to the displaced and brokenhearted while carrying his own deep and abiding grief. I read every word Tony writes, and I am changed."

—**Dr. Donna K. Wallace**,
New York Times bestselling author

"This book…sure looks promising as a valuable life navigation tool. I simply place my order now. Get me the rest of the book… the day it is released. I am a businessman of 35 years, working with many, many people…Through the decades I have read and compiled a large personal library of Christian-authored books. It is both a personal hobby and a source of 'tools' in time of need or curiosity stemming from our company's belief in developing a 'learning culture' through reading. We know that a solid book can prompt growth in life, both personal and business. …This book, in my opinion, will prove to be one of those solid books. It will be located right on my desk, for that 'day' of disruption, for myself or my friends."

—**Ross Hall**, International Marketing Director.

"In this book Tony Nelson adds another critical perspective to the continuing education of all of us who suffer or seek to comfort those who do. But the key terms that struck a chord with me in his contribution were "navigating" and "hope." Tony speaks from a long history of experience and a deep understanding of Scripture as he comes along side of us in our path through suffering and pain while helping us to actually, not just theoretically, keep hope alive. These are words of comfort but they are also words of instruction. I doubt if anyone reading this book will walk away in the same state of mind and heart that they had in opening to the first page. This book will help you grow."

—**Dr. Boyd Hannold**, Lead Pastor
Princeton Alliance Church

"This impactful book is part Paul Harvey's *The Rest of the Story*, part Ravi Zacharias' *Let My People Think* delivered in a captivating Max Lucado's pictorial writing style. *Crazy Life* is an out-of-the-box work that taps the intellect emphasizing God's very deliberate hand in the crazy part of our lives; all twists, turns, triumphs and tragedies show Him in the center of our lives, like the eye of a hurricane, making us stronger, bolder, and more dependent on Him with biblical heroes to prove it! Dr. Nelson's descriptive analogies combined with his raw, personal life references draw readers into a deeper contemplation of the inferences that may exist between scriptural verses. Tony weaves together a wonderful word-picture of hope for the hurting and a sharper glimpse of a God who is always working behind the scenes. Thanks Tony for helping believers to question and think!"

—Heather Mehra-Pedersen,
Co-founder BookCrossing, Inc. and
Director Asia International Children's Network

crazy
LIFE

Navigating Through Life's
DISRUPTIONS
Without Losing Your Faith

Dr. TONY L. NELSON

NEW YORK

NASHVILLE MELBOURNE

crazy LIFE
Navigating Through Life's DISRUPTIONS
Without Losing Your Faith

© 2017 Dr. TONY L. NELSON

Published in New York, New York, by Morgan James Publishing. Morgan James and The Entrepreneurial Publisher are trademarks of Morgan James, LLC.
www.MorganJamesPublishing.com

The Morgan James Speakers Group can bring authors to your live event. For more information or to book an event visit The Morgan James Speakers Group at www.TheMorganJamesSpeakersGroup.com.
Scripture quotations, unless otherwise noted, are from the HOLY BIBLE: NEW INTERNATIONAL VERSION. Copyright 2011 by The International Bible Society. The author has added italics to Scripture quotations for emphasis.

Shelfie

A **free** eBook edition is available with the purchase of this print book.

CLEARLY PRINT YOUR NAME ABOVE IN UPPER CASE

Instructions to claim your free eBook edition:
1. Download the Shelfie app for Android or iOS
2. Write your name in **UPPER CASE** above
3. Use the Shelfie app to submit a photo
4. Download your eBook to any device

ISBN 978-1-68350-212-8 paperback
ISBN 978-1-68350-213-5 eBook
ISBN 978-1-68350-214-2 hardcover
Library of Congress Control Number:
2016914262

Cover Design by:
Rachel Lopez
www.r2cdesign.com

Interior Design by:
Bonnie Bushman
The Whole Caboodle Graphic Design

Morgan James
The Entrepreneurial Publisher™

Builds

with...

Habitat for Humanity®
Peninsula and
Greater Williamsburg

In an effort to support local communities, raise awareness and funds, Morgan James Publishing donates a percentage of all book sales for the life of each book to Habitat for Humanity Peninsula and Greater Williamsburg.

Get involved today! Visit
www.MorganJamesBuilds.com

*To all those whose lives have been disrupted
and redeemed for the Glory of God,
for their ultimate good and
for the sake of the world.*

Contents

Acknowledgments

This book was born out of the fiery crucible of life. My life, my wife's life, our extended family's lives and that of hundreds of others with whom we have journeyed together over the years. The doubts, struggles, fears and tears that come to all of us tilled the soil from which this book of brutal honesty and outrageous hope grew. Some days the words flew onto the page. Other days, I had to walk away from the keyboard when the computer screen became blurred from the tears that came with many memories; happy tears and sad tears, but tears nonetheless. That's why God gave us two eye-ducts, right?

When friends and even strangers found out I was writing a book they would ask me what the title was. I would always say, "Crazy Life." With few exceptions they would say something like, "Wow, I can't wait to get a copy because that describes my life right now—crazy!"

So many people enthusiastically encouraged me to write this Christian view of disruption. At the risk of missing the many who were instrumental in getting this book released to the world, I am going to name a few of the men and women to whom I am indebted and in some way express my gratitude for their influence in my life. I want to express my gratitude to:

Jesus, my Redeemer: I love you and thank you for redeeming all the things in my life for the Father's glory, my ultimate good and for the sake of the world.

First Christian Church in Sandpoint, Idaho: It was truly a privilege to have served and loved you for over 22 years. We were family. God shaped both of us as we walked together through the triumphs and tragedies of this life and made disciples of Jesus.

Sandpoint Pastor's Network: What a privilege it was to be part of a band of brothers that stood with me through the long up-and-down journey of ministry in a small town. I cherish our annual prayer summits where we met Jesus and discovered one another's hearts. Sandpoint has been enriched because of you.

The men and women who have shared their journeys with me: I am honored to have been called your pastor, your friend and your brother in Christ. Your stories are woven into the pages of this book for only one reason: to help others stay the course.

All my dear friends and family members who have been praying for me: Without your covering, this project would not have been finished. More importantly, your love and prayers guided me through that long season of disbelief and brought me home like a Prodigal.

George Fox Seminary: Thank you professors and administrators for making such an enriching and challenging degree program available to those of us on the front lines of ministry. Thanks to the three different cohorts with whom I rubbed shoulders in the two years of our time together at Cannon Beach. I am better for the diversity of backgrounds and ideas.

Dr. Donna K. Wallace, my book-architect extraordinaire: Without your encouragement from the earliest days of editing my dissertation—*Redeeming Disruptions*—to the formation of *Communitas* as a writing community, to our present writing journey, this book would have never happened. You saw what I didn't—that people needed to know what God said about interruption *and* that I was the messenger of hope.

James Wallace: Thanks for letting Donna spread hard copies of my manuscript all over your house. I owe you a visit to the driving range for that.

Don Otis, a friend in the publishing world: Your referrals at a time when I had come to so many dead ends kept my book proposal alive until it landed in the right hands. I am deeply grateful.

Terry Whalin, my acquisition agent: Thank you for taking Don's referral to read a book proposal from an unpublished author and actually reading it! Your later phone call congratulating me for getting picked up by Morgan James Publishing still ranks up there as one of the happiest experiences of my adult life. You should have seen the happy dance!

David Hancock, founder of Morgan James Publishing: Thanks for starting a company that values authors, even unpublished ones. I believe this book will reward your business acumen as well as help many people experience Christ in a significant way.

Margo Toulouse, my Managing Editor: Your professionalism, ongoing encouragement and recommendations made this book a top shelf product that we can all be proud of. Thank you.

My volunteer proof-readers: Tasha Cropper, Stetson McElhaney, Martin Flaherty, Troy Burns, Heather Mehera-Pedersen and Charis Uzabel. You did a fantastic job putting the finishing touches on this book. Thanks!

Geek (Erik), my brother-"no good"-in-law: Thanks for letting me call you when I got writer's block or needed a distraction. You always made me laugh and told me to go back to work. I did, and here's the proof.

My son Craig, my daughter Carlina, and son-in-law Adam: Your words of encouragement and belief in me helped me finish my dissertation, which became the foundation of this book. This is our book for people just like us; and there are a lot of them.

Disa, my beloved wife: Your yellow sticky note that reads, "Keep writing! People need to hear what you have to say! U Can do it!" hangs on my monitor as a reminder that this is our book, born out of life experiences and three decades of marriage and ministry. Your enthusiasm for this book became my source of inspiration to press on. This book is our beacon of light for many caught in the darkness of disruption. I love you the "most-est!"

Introduction

Every life gets interrupted. Some disruptions are irritating, others tragic, and some even come from good life experiences, such as the birth of a child. The problem is that few of us actually prepare, practice, or make ready for life's storms. As a result, sometimes our faith begins to erode like a river bank when the floodwaters of life rise too high.

One day when my own circumstances were at flood stage, I sat down on a log in the woods and asked myself, or God, or whatever other wild beast was close enough to listen: *What would happen if a dad or mom (or a single person) actually prepared one's family for times of chaos?* Noah did. What would happen in a community if Christ's followers actually prepared safe places for others to weather life's typhoons? I believe, we too, would have a full ark.

I opened my Bible when I got home and re-read the famous story. I didn't find the cute, cartoonish animals going into a giant, odd-shaped boat, two-by-two, with a rainbow tucked between puffy clouds. What I found was a man responding to God's call. The part of the story that grabbed my attention was that Noah and God shared such a close relationship that Noah trusted God's provision for an absolutely crazy future. He relied fully on God's instructions while preparing for the upcoming catastrophe. You, too, can turn to the pages of God's Story to discover the value of planning and preparation as valuable tools in navigating "high waters." In these pages you will:

- Find that interruption is part of God's divine plan and can be embraced for positive life change.
- Learn effective ways to steer through the chaos of life's speed bumps and grow in your own faith through the process.
- Be able to help guide others who are struggling with life's trials to a deeper understanding of their purpose and faith in God.

You will find that *you're not crazy; life is*! We are not left to negotiate the storm alone or to fend for ourselves. In fact, I believe that chaos is utilized in God's own plan to draw us closer to Him. Throughout this book there will be several key life principles taken from the Scriptures that can become waypoints for you as you navigate your own life interruptions and challenges. They are as follows:

Disruptions are normal. Many Christians suffer from life's unforeseen and challenging scenarios. Western Christians especially seem surprised that life is hard. Is this God's discipline? Is God withholding His blessing? Is this a test? Much of our mental anguish that we experience while going through hard times is the result of a defective theology of disruption. We simply have no understanding that God's plan for our lives involves disruptive experiences. In addition, many believers have not been adequately taught biblical principles and practices to help guide them through these difficulties. We need to to know that we can grow in our faith by finding God in the interruptions.

Disruptions can be successfully navigated and can even make us stronger. If we are to grow in our faith through life's intervals of mayhem, we will need to understand the principles and characteristics of those who have gone before us and successfully maneuvered through a crazy life. Eight ancient character studies from the Bible are coupled with contemporary life stories. Step into the stories of your most beloved Bible characters: Adam and Eve, Job, Abraham, Elijah, Mary the mother of Jesus, Peter, Paul and Jesus, to see their own challenges from a whole new perspective.

Disruptions are the "stuff" of which successful leaders, spouses, parents, children and neighbors are made. What is more essential than learning to grow through one's own trials? What's more important than becoming the kind of person who knows hope in great upset or becoming one who feasts at the table spread before one's enemies during the struggle? What do we find at God's table? We find the Fruit of the Spirit: love, joy, peace, patience and so forth (Gal. 5:22-23). Only when we see God's perspective and receive God's nurturance can we, like Christ, say, "This peace I give you, this peace I leave with you," and invite others to sit at the table with us. The Bible is full of incredible—crazy stories. How did God insure Adam would embrace Eve? What was Abraham thinking when he took the senior citizens' tour of Ancient Palestine?

If you are either currently in, or have gone through, a difficult time, or know someone who is struggling with his or her faith as a result of hijacked plans, this book is for you. Are you committed to personal and spiritual growth, even after having experienced an untimely death, divorce, job promotion or birth of a child? If you have stopped asking "Where is God when it hurts?" but rather start asking, "How can this possibly be God's plan and what am I supposed to be doing if it is?" If you are looking for help in knowing how to press into the heart of God, I invite you to this profound journey. What if disruption was God's original intent for growing us? How would it help us today to know that God can and will redeem any and all intrusive interludes, whatever the source? As we'll see in God's timeless story of His coming and His great, enduring love, God is not surprised by our brokenness and the bad decisions that we make. In fact, disruption is God's *normal method* of forming us and drawing us to Himself as revealed in the bible from Adam in Genesis to Jesus in Revelation.

Crazy Life proposes the solution first: God uses interruption as the normal way to grow His children. Then it illustrates, through story, how God's intentions apply to problem situations. Regardless of how we feel, we are not abandoned in life's detours and train wrecks. Every Christian experiences crazy times in life, to varying degrees of intensity, but few believers are prepared to stay a course successfully through life's upheavals. As a result, even the most solid leaders have been known to falter in their faith (or lose it all together) and therefore miss out on personal and/or organizational growth experiences inherent in the interruptive challenges themselves. The purpose of this book is to equip Christians to successfully navigate through life's crazy intermissions without losing their faith…and find hope in the journey.

You won't want to miss, Book II in the Crazy Life series:

Crazy Leadership
Uncovering Timeless Leadership Principles
that Bring Crazy Results

In *Crazy Leadership,* I will unpack biblical characters who modeled insane leadership feats. Nehemiah rebuilt the walls of Jerusalem in 100 days: Jonah pulled a big geographic in the wrong direction, yet still changed an entire city. The Apostle Peter "failed forward" to become a pillar of the early church. The Apostle Paul, was a murderer-turned-author. Wherever you're in your leadership journey, you're sure to find camaraderie in these biblical characters and timeless principles.

Chapter One

Adam's Scar

Divine Disruption In Paradise

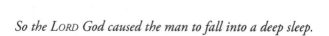

So the LORD God caused the man to fall into a deep sleep.
Genesis 2:21

From humanity's very beginning in Genesis, we find the story where God interrupts Adam's life, causing pain and discomfort, so that He can present a handcrafted solution to Adam's need in the person of Eve. God used disruption to form and shape Adam (and Eve) and to draw them into a trusting relationship. Disruption has always been a part of God's plan to spiritually form all humanity—even before the Fall.

1

The autumn colors were spectacular out the windows of the Chevy Tahoe the day my long time elk-hunting buddy, Paul, and I were descending a steep mountain grade. Our mood was as bright as the noonday sun that ignited stands of brilliant golds and reds across the mountainside. While bouncing down the rough backwoods road, we were engaged in typical manly small talk—It sure is great to be out! Where's the elk? ...So, the family's good?—then, like one of the switchbacks we were navigating, our conversation took a quick turn into the deeper stuff of life.

I told Paul about this book and he was curious. I gave him the elevator speech version and expressed my belief that the book would help people navigating life's disruptions without losing their faith. Paul got silent and I could see his far-off gaze; I knew he was no longer seeing brightly colored Tamarack and Aspen trees. Another scene was playing through his mind. The idea of life's disruptions and keeping one's faith was not merely an interesting concept for my friend. My mention of it triggered a life-altering memory for Paul—the tragic death of his first wife, Maryann. I felt my throat tighten and I laid a hand on Paul's shoulder. In the silence, we remembered together that fateful day, July 27, 2002, when he called to tell me that his wife was fighting for her life.

I remembered that July day Paul was traveling to a nearby town when he fielded a call from his anesthesia partner. His partner told him about Maryann's admittance to the Emergency Room. Paul's many years in private anesthesia practice caused him to realize this was a life-threatening situation for Maryann, his wife and best friend for over thirty years. This was totally unexpected and came with no warning. She had been in good health, and now she was fighting for her life.

I had sat at Maryann's dinner table many times, often having just come from the woods with her husband—my hunting buddy—in dirty camo clothing, and she still treated me like I was royalty! She was a great hostess, wife, mother and Christian. You would have liked her. Paul called me and I dropped everything. I sped to the ER as both pastor and friend. Paul was standing outside of the Emergency Room of Sandpoint's local hospital where he stoically updated me on the seriousness of the situation. He said things were not going well for Maryann. Moments trudged by as the medical team worked to save her life. We prayed. We paced. We begged God for a miracle. She didn't make it. For some reason, unexplained even after a post-mortem autopsy, Maryann died from an internal bleed that couldn't be located. It didn't make sense then. It doesn't make sense now.

"She was fit and so full of life, Tony."

"I know," I said about that traumatic, life-altering moment. "That was a crazy day. It was the last thing I ever thought we'd have to go through together. Neither one of us were ready to say goodbye to Maryann."

With a voice choked by an unexpected surge of grief, Paul shared how the memory of Maryann's death still makes him weep…even all these years later. Such moments stop us in our tracks, or more accurately, they push us onto a new set of tracks that we have never traveled on before. After a long pause, guiding the truck down the rough mountain grade, my friend looked over at me and said with a whisper, "What a difference a day makes, eh?"

That is what this book is about, *the difference a day makes*. What a difference that one event—on one given day—in one moment of time—makes, and not one of us is left untouched. In my role of friend and pastor, I look into tear-stained faces asking me how to make sense of such days and the path that stretches out ahead. These events don't necessarily have to be tragic as described above. They can be good things: the birth of a child, a wedding, a promotion; but what they share in common is *disruption*.

I've listened to mothers who face an empty nest, couples experiencing a move to an unfamiliar city, and those in the exhausting start-up years of a new business. I am not untouched. God has seemingly taken me through, yea, dragged me, kicking and squirming, into death-filled valleys where I felt utterly weary and abandoned. I've rushed to too many Emergency Rooms and later stood by too many freshly dug graves of infants, youth, and adults. These graves became spiritual markers in my quest to understand the mystery and seeming aloofness of God.

After several decades in ministry, I finally ran out of nicely packaged statements about life and death. My neatly "borrowed" theologies and attached "creedal statements" began to smell no better than a bad can of tuna. I found myself not knowing what to say to my friends, family and parishioners when they needed me most—in the throes of life's hardships. What was I supposed to tell them? Looking back with more clarity now, I see that my own crisis of faith journey had me walking a path of agnosticism pointed straight toward the cliff of atheism. It's not a good place for anyone to be, let alone me, a vocational minister of the gospel.

I was supposed to be the answer guy for life's big questions. Instead, God's silence began to eat away at my soul like rust on a truck fender and I found myself tossing out old, worn Christian clichés. Whether you are a person who follows the Christian faith or not, if you've experienced hard times, you, too, have heard more than your share. We hate clichés, but they abound because we feel the need to say something in an attempt to comfort the disrupted. Here are a few we should avoid like The Plague:

1. "Where God guides He provides."
   How many times have you heard about a failed business because someone thought that God was guiding him or her to make some significant financial investment? Yeah, this rhymes, but it doesn't "hold a tune" to the true biblical stories of God working in people's lives, who're sometimes incredibly foolish.

2. "If God brings you to it, He will bring you through it."

   Here's another rhyming catch phrase that really doesn't explain anything. What if you brought yourself "to it," or the "bringing you through it" part takes 20 years?

3. "When God closes a door, He opens a window."

   What does this really mean other than, "God changed His mind and now you've got to crawl through a window?"

4. "Man meant it for evil, but God meant it for good."

   So is God now responsible for evil? I will address this later by pointing out that Scripture clearly teaches that God can redeem evil (i.e. the restoration of Job). More importantly, I'll consistently point out the truth that we rarely know the cause of our disruptions because we live in a fallen world.

5. "God must have needed another angel in heaven, that is why your loved one just died."

   This one really gets me hot. What nonsense, really. The Bible *never* suggests that this actually happens.

6. "God is Sovereign; we're not supposed to question His ways—ever. Just believe." [1]

   If I've discovered anything about God lately it is that He welcomes the hard questions. This seems to be a statement that swirls around in some denominations more readily than others. Pushed to extreme, this view of God's Sovereignty actually makes Him responsible for evil. Not a good place to land… especially when enduring great suffering.

No doubt you can add to the list. I don't know about you, but I couldn't stomach the clichés any longer. I had become deeply disappointed in God's track record. It seemed that God stopped listening to my prayers. I had become weary of untimely deaths, divorce, and people just behaving badly. I prayed and nothing seemed to change.

The Genesis of Disruption

By vocation, I am invited into the lives of people who experience interruptions of varying intensities. It is my job to help bring peace, a sense of purpose, or at least God's presence at a difficult time. I have observed that when people's lives are disrupted—including people of faith—they usually default to the ancient lament of humanity, "Why is life so hard? It shouldn't be this way!"

It made me wonder: Is all of life's craziness, good or bad, the result of human decision and a fallen world? If God is so good, what did God have in mind when He created the world that ended up like it is today, filled with disruptive processes and experiences? Most of my mental anguish can be boiled down to this one question: *Are disruptions and their accompanying challenges part of God's Divine plan?*

This question, and my own lack of understanding, led to a crisis of faith. I found myself filled with soul-numbing angst. Looking back, I admit that sometimes my angst gave way like old ice crumbling away from a shore line, to utter disgust in God's perceived performance—which prompted yelling sessions with the Almighty. It is my sincere hope these "prayers" have not been recorded for all eternity like the Psalms!

A deeper theological question I've wrestled with goes like this, "What was God's original plan to draw us into relationship with Him, without violating our human free-will?" I believe God has a plan. I believe that we have free will. What this chapter and this book will explore is the powerful role that disruption plays in God's plan for our lives. A plan that brings Him glory, grows us as human beings and ultimately blesses the world.

Drawn Deeper through Interruption

I want to help you journey through your own personal disruptions. This book weaves together real life and biblical stories so we can begin to develop a "theology of disruption." You won't find trite answers here. Instead these chapters serve as a guide. I want to help you understand and embrace the positive, life shaping power of these unexpected, re-directing experiences for your own good, as well as the good of others. Life, when understood through our personal and biblical stories, is a journey of discovering the ways God uses the energy of disruption to personally shape us into His vision for good.

In addition, I want to help you see God *in* the interruption. Notice that I didn't say God *causes* the disruption. There's plenty of biblical evidence to suggest that God does as He so chooses, as with Noah and the Great Flood. The stark reality is that we won't always know who or what causes a disruption.

On a personal level, I discovered that the book of Genesis was, and still is, an amazing place to go with the hard questions of life. This first book of the Bible cleared up some of the fog that entrapped me as I attempted to understand the role of disruption in life. For me, this book of origins was like going back to the blueprints of a master-planned community to discover God-the-Architect's ideas and concepts.

Disruption in Paradise

In Genesis, we find the story of origins, how this inhabited planet, as well as the entire universe, came to be. Genesis tells us clearly that we are created on purpose. We are God's grand design, the epitome of God's creative force. Therefore, we can learn much about God's original design and plan for us by studying the book of beginnings.

We also find resolution to many of our questions in the book of Genesis. You may already be skimming this section, thinking, "Yeah, I've read Genesis a dozen times." Hold on a second. Has it ever occurred to you that the Master Creator, God Himself, staged the ultimate Divine disruption in the opening story of humanity? Have you noticed how in the perfect setting, on a perfect day, God called a monumental "Time

Out" for our perfect parents—especially Adam—*BEFORE THE FALL?* I'm getting ahead of myself.

"Time Out" in the Garden

Indulge me for a moment as we re-establish the foundation of the story that builds to the climactic "Time Out." One of the foundational truths of Genesis is that in the very beginning everything was good. God was good. The earth was good. Adam was good. Genesis clearly states God's view of His work; "God saw all that he had made, and it was very good" (Gen. 1:31). "Very good," not just so-so, or close-enough-for-government-work, but exceedingly good—in a word, Paradise. Not only were God's creatures incredible, they were in an amazingly GOOD place! Theirs was a good world crafted by a good God filled with good things.

This ancient text reminds us that *it was God* who "planted a garden in the east of Eden" (Gen. 2:8). Not only did God create, He *shaped* the very environment where He placed his masterpiece—Adam. "The Lord God took the man and put him in the Garden of Eden to work it and take care of it" (Gen. 2:15). The Master Creator gave Adam His creative best as a place to not just live, but to live with purpose, "to work and take care of it."; dare I say, "to thrive."

To what do we compare Eden? Maybe Eden is the feeling we get when we grab a brochure off a tourist cache with a picture of a white sandy beach in Maui. The water is aquamarine blue with light surf gently caressing the shore. In your mind's eye you can see yourself standing there digging your bare toes into this tropical island's volcanic warmth. The smile that breaks out on your face gives away your thought that "Maui would be a fantastic place to be right now—like paradise."

It stands to reason then, that in Eden, God's interaction with His creatures was *also* good, right? Let's skip ahead in time. We don't know how long it was between Genesis 1:31 and 2:18, but the next part of the

Creation Narrative is powerful in that it will show us that from the very beginning *God used disruption to form and shape Adam (and Eve) and to draw them into a trusting relationship.* Don't miss how God was *in* the disruption and notice how active God is *in* the story.

Not Every Thing was Good

After creating the world and Adam, God and His creation seem to be having a wonderful time. Then, in verse 18, for the first time in the creation story God says somethin is not good. "It is not good for the man to be alone" (Gen. 2:18). Prior to this, everything was good, even "very good." Here, Genesis gives up an interesting secret that is often missed. Notice how God announces that there was something in Adam's life that was not good, even before Adam himself recognized it. Don't miss the fact that our Creator knows us—intimately. He knows us better than we know ourselves. Thus, God alone, our Master Designer, knows what is "not good" in our lives or current environment.

> God alone, our Master Designer, knows what is "not good" in our lives or current environment.

This is the foundational principle and the bedrock of this book: God, and God alone, knows what we need *and only He knows* how to meet that need. God doesn't need us to take a personality profile, or a spiritual gift inventory, or to go through a battery of psychological tests to discover these things. They enlighten us, but God is already "in the know." God knows every nook and cranny of our lives. Great Designer that He is, He alone knows what we need, what we can and cannot do, what our stress loads are and what makes us tick. God, the Great Psychologist, knows the complexity of our emotions, our motives and our drives. God, the Great Physician, knows our health needs and can anticipate where our current dietary habits might lead us. God, our Spiritual Director, sees the whole person: body, mind and spirit. He alone has the ability to address our complicated needs with divine solutions. Not only does God redeem stressful interruptions and losses, disruption is part of God's original plan.

More specifically, God knows what is best for us *before we do*. You can call God the "Great Anticipator". You might say that God is constantly working upstream on our behalf. We can only see the water passing by that's right in front of us. It is water that has already been touched by God. The Genesis record doesn't show us a God who creates and leaves, but rather a loving Father who pursues a relationship with Adam and Eve and their offspring up to this very moment. He never gave up on them. He never gives up on us. God continues to actively invest Himself in the redemption and spiritual formation of humanity for their good and to bless the entire world.

At this point in the story, the plot gets really interesting. God identifies a need (that Adam is completely unaware of), so God sets about to create a moment in time when Adam *will feel* that need and hopefully turn to his Maker for solution. What God does next is staggering. For most of my adult life I missed this picture of Divine disruption presented so beautifully in the pages of Genesis. Yet Genesis clearly portrays this amazing truth: *God is about to step into Adam's perfect little world and disrupt it.* Let's dig deeper.

First, The Great Anticipator assigns Adam the mundane task of naming all the "wild animals and all the birds of the sky" (Gen. 2:19). Notice how active God is *in* this story. God "brought them to the man to see what he would name them; and whatever the man called each living creature, that was its name." To press my point further, Adam was essentially clueless. He probably got a huge kick out of seeing all the creatures that God had "formed out of the ground" and found it intellectually stimulating to come up with names. Imagine trying to come up with the name for a mammal that has the bill of a duck and the tail of a beaver—a Platypus—of course! Then there came the giraffe, the gazelle and the elk; creature after creature, strange and magnificent, paraded by. Adam thought he was just naming, but God had a greater purpose in this assignment, a higher purpose if you will—to create an environment where Adam would receive Eve with abandon. Together, they would launch humanity—populating the world, fulfilling God's original purpose for creating this blue planet.

This little story-within-a-story, helps us become aware of the activity of God. It shows us that God brings "experiences and opportunities" into our lives—like the animals were to Adam—events that are designed to take us further down the path of self-discovery and growth.

Adam embraced the day. He named the animals. He studied them. Then all of a sudden, in the midst of this Divine exercise, he makes a brilliant "self-discovery." The writer of Genesis describes, "But for Adam, no suitable helper was found" (Gen. 2:20). *The Message*[2] translates it this way, "but he didn't find a suitable companion." It would be fair and accurate to say that Adam discovered that he was alone—completely alone—in Eden. There was no other creature like him. I suggest that this realization was life-altering. Possibly for the first time, Adam became aware of a need. Perfect man felt something that was not good: *aloneness*. Don't forget, God created the environment in which Adam would become aware of his need.

Not only was God the causal agent of Adam's need, God takes the initiative to meet that need: "So the Lord God caused the man to fall into a deep sleep; and while he was sleeping, he took one of the man's ribs and then closed up the place with flesh" (Gen. 2:21). God put Adam to sleep and then opened up Adam's side—surgically removing a rib. Adam ended up

> **This experience had to create some pain and suffering on Adam's part— *before* he saw Eve.**

with a scar. I want to take some poetic license here and suggest, as a man and as a human, this experience had to create some pain and suffering on Adam's part—before he saw Eve. My argument is based on human physiology. Adam was engineered with nerve endings, just like we have, so his post-operative experience surely included pain. The removal of the rib and the following recovery must have made breathing and coughing hurt. Nowhere in the Genesis record does its author, Moses, state that early humanity lacked the ability to experience pain. As a matter of fact, later in Genesis God tells Eve, "and your pain in childbirth will increase"—presupposing that there was pain in childbirth prior to the Fall.

I've visited many people in the hospital who had a surgery that required a rib to be pulled aside or removed and every one of these people hurt after the fact. Arguing from the silence of Scripture suggests that when Adam woke up missing a rib, he was in discomfort. Who caused it? God did. God interrupted Adam's life for the good; for the good of Adam, for the good of humanity (you wouldn't be reading this if Eve hadn't shown up), and for the good of the earth. Let me emphasize; God was fully *in* this first recorded disruption.

It is helpful to see how this divine interruption plays out for Adam. Genesis says, "Then the Lord God made a woman from the rib he had taken out of man, and he brought her to the man" (Gen. 2:27). Notice the crazy love that God shows Adam by making and bringing him another creature specifically designed for him alone. Adam went through the disruptive process to be greeted by the crown of creation—woman.

Notice how he responds. "The man said, 'This is now bone of my bones and flesh of my flesh; she shall be called 'woman,' for she was taken out of man'" (Gen. 2:23). Lest we miss the awe and wonder in his proclamation, Adam was stoked! Whatever discomfort God caused was quickly forgotten and forgiven!

What stood before Adam was this amazing creature that fit him perfectly and made things good again in his life. Moses, the writer of Genesis, adds this commentary to the event by referencing the drawing power of woman upon man; "That is why a man leaves his father and mother and is united to his wife, and they become one flesh" (Gen. 2:24). God's provision for Adam's need—Eve—fit him so completely that this Bible chapter concludes by stating that "Adam and his wife were both naked, and they felt no shame" (Gen. 2:25). Eve was God's perfect solution to Adam's problem.

Adam, like my friend Paul, might have also said, "What a difference a day makes, eh?"

God's Good Plan

It is critical that we have way-points to help us navigate life's interruptions. My GPS device makes it possible for me to punch a button while hiking in the woods so that I can find my way back. I always make a way-point for my truck's location so that if I get lost in the Idaho mountains, I can navigate my way back to my truck— my home base—using this way-point. Genesis gives us our home-base way-point. We return to our story of beginnings again and again; the story of a loving God Who has our best in mind as He fashions experiences to both grow us as people and to draw us closer to Him in relationship. If we miss this point of navigation, then we will find ourselves wandering around the great woodlands of life blaming God for getting us lost.

There is hope in this beautiful love story. Right now, wherever you are in your life journey, God is working for your good. There is One who knows your need and is "all in," working to bring you something of beauty and wonder—your own "Eve"—a birthing of something you cannot yet think of or imagine. Furthermore, I'm convinced the process will take place the same as Adam's did, through divine disruption.

Why? Because the Genesis record shows us that purposeful disruption was God's plan from the very beginning; before the Fall. Before the forbidden fruit was plucked, God, had established a process to grow us for good. That hasn't changed. God knows, He anticipates, He disrupts, and He provides.

Like Adam, we can either accept the process as normal and embrace our Creator's solution, or shake our fist and accuse God of not being good. Our wrestling with God and His plan for our lives is to be expected. After all, the Bible tells us God named one of the great Patriarchs, "Israel", which means "wrestling." Do you think God was trying to communicate something intrinsic to all future generations about Himself and his plans with this moniker?

Learning anew from Genesis that God is good and that His plans are good, albeit mysterious at times, pushed back the fog of doubt in my mind and uprooted the seedlings of unbelief that had taken root in my heart. I reasoned, if God is truly good, then I can trust my Creator's presence in the disruptive processes and experiences of my life.

This discovery in the story of beginnings led me away from the abyss of atheism. While it didn't make the pain of disruptive forces any less, it did give me a perspective in this journey we call life. If God disrupted Adam's life, then I, too, can embrace this as a necessary reality in my relationship with God. If I want to have a moment in time when I get to experience an "Eve-like" solution, then I need to trust God before, during, and after this process of being spiritually formed through disruption.

I began this chapter by sharing a very private moment with my dear friend Paul. Paul's world was wrecked when Maryann passed away for unknown medical reasons. His dreams of growing old with the love of his life were shattered. Death snatched his soul mate. I got a front row seat to his journey through the valley of the shadow of death. We continued to hunt together in the fall and catch an occasional summer day fishing the waters of beautiful Lake Pend Oreille in Idaho. There were days when I saw that he was making great progress in his grief recovery. Then there were those other days when I saw that his grief weighted him down like an ancient millstone hanging around his neck.

The details of Paul's journey are his to tell, but I've been given permission to mention he rode through this season of life without losing his faith. As a matter of fact, God brought him an "Eve," a loving and caring wife, all the way from Jakarta, Indonesia. Now happily remarried and living a purposeful life, Paul didn't let death's disruption break his spirit or destroy his faith. He wept. He laughed. He prayed and worshipped, letting God guide and direct his steps. Did he do it perfectly? No. No one does. As you already know, there are days when the "dogs of grief" demand attention.

What a difference a day makes.

Maybe this day, this present "right now" while you hold this book in your hands, is an affirmation that God is busy redeeming your disruptions. You are not alone. God is also inviting you to wait on His provision as Adam did for Eve.

Questions for Discussion

1. Describe a time when your life was disrupted for good or bad.
2. On a scale of 1-5, 1 being "really far away" and 5 being "really close," how would you measure your current relationship with God? Please explain your answer.
3. Can you relate to the author's story of "going down the path of agnosticism toward the cliff of atheism." Can you relate or not? Explain.
4. What are some common Christian clichés that people have used during a challenging period of your life? What was your reaction to them?

5. Explain in your own words the author's claim that God is IN the interruptions.

6. Describe a time when God provided for your needs—beyond the bounds of your own personal performance. How did it come about? Was the answer/solution what you originally sought?

Chapter Two

Eve's Embrace

Designed On Purpose
For The Sake Of Others

"You don't know how beautiful you are"
—Bono

What happens when women realize that they were created to be world-class problem solvers? "Eve's Embrace" will reveal that a woman is by nature created to transform the world.

T he "crazy" of this broken world affects every human being, yet some of the worst atrocities and longest lasting oppression ever wrought throughout history wreaked havoc on the lives of women and children. Likewise, some of the world's best, most creative innovators are also women and children. Because of this, I want to give special attention to the rest of the Creation story. The first recorded disruption in God's plan – *this indomitable, creative force we call "woman,"* – was fashioned with breathtaking beauty and profound purpose. God had a plan that included her from the very beginning: she, would be united with the first man, and together they reflect the glorious "image of God" (Gen. 1:27).

Other biblical characters have been lauded as heroes and looked to for leadership models throughout Jewish and Christian history. Little has been written about Eve that portrays the first woman's positive traits. Instead, Eve receives most of the blame for the fall of humanity, being the first one to break God's only rule. But, to fully appreciate Eve's world-changing design, let's look in the rearview mirror and take another look at the person and work of Eve before the Fall…when she was still just a gleam in her Father's eye.

Eve's Goodness

Let's re-visit the Garden of Eden. Adam was still child-like in his trust, running and skipping in awe and wonder at the trees and the beasts and the streams teaming with the most gorgeous fish. Each day he was making new and astounding discoveries in Paradise… It was all sooo good! Yet, at the end of the day, he lay down with a bit of a gnawing ache in his gut.

As mentioned in Chapter One, the only thing that God said *was not good* was Adam's aloneness. Here we see how God addresses Adam's problem without violating his free will. God, the Great Anticipator, set about doing something amazing; God was at work solving a massive human dilemma.

Instead of taking the direct approach, God took the longer road of letting Adam discover for himself that things were not altogether right. God could have taken a rib from Adam any time he wanted, fashioned a woman, and presented her. He didn't. God waited for the right time and the right moment when Adam was ready for the solution. We don't know how much time passed, but it would be accurate to say that there was a season of Adam's life where he experienced a holy discontent that morphed into a felt need.So we have the first human, Adam, sensing that all was not right with his world. Adam was right where God wanted him *because God crafted this moment in time.* But interestingly enough (and contrary to popular leadership philosophy), God doesn't empower Adam to meet his own need.

What might have happened had Adam tried to solve his own need? I can imagine a Frankenstein-ian result if God had directed Adam to "go make yourself a 'helpmate'" to alleviate his loneliness. What would Adam have conjured up? He was now the universal expert on animals, having just spent a good amount of time in Biology 101, naming the animals. It's creepy to think that he might have taken a bunch of different animal concepts and created something in his own image.

A Gift for Adam

Adam lacked the ability and vision to figure out a solution to his problem of having no counterpart. God must have been giddy about his future surprise; the Great Anticipator's solution was so far beyond Adam's experience and ability to reason. And yet, when God acted, the Creator required Adam to be vested in the solution—by giving up a part of his perfect body—a rib.

We don't know if they discussed this beforehand or if Adam was surprised by the whole experience. The silence of Scripture would lead me to believe that Adam willingly allowed himself to experience divine anesthesia and "go under the knife" as a patient would with a skilled surgeon. His first recorded words after the fact weren't, "Ouch that hurt" but, "bone of my bone." God invited Adam to make a significant sacrifice, I think, so that he would have ownership in the solution.

Every May in Sandpoint, ID they have a vintage car event and parade that I usually attended. Hundreds of vintage cars show up from all over the Northwest to be seen and heard. Walking streets that are filled with vintage '57 Chevy's and '65 Mustangs, I can usually tell from the demeanor of the owner whether the car was "bought" or "built." A built car requires the owner to invest a lot of time, money and skin to restore his or her beauty. A bought car reflects only the sacrifice of money. On one hand, the built car's owner can tell you all the details of where he found that fender and how he rebuilt the engine. On the other, the bought car owner just wipes the dust off the hood and sometimes doesn't know much about that particular car. You get the picture. Adam had skin in the game.

God takes a rib and makes woman. Every woman on this planet traces her origins to this moment in time, a specially crafted and designed human being to make all that is not good, into something very good. And not only that, God graced the world with the heart-stopping presence of a woman.

I am an avid outdoorsman. I love to hunt and fish and play outside in God's wonderful creation. In the summer you can find me fly fishing a mountain stream trying to fool a native born trout with a tuft of feathers and yarn (the fly). When I catch one, I will often hold the torpedo-shaped fish in my hands and gaze at its incredible design and beauty. I still marvel at a rainbow trout's brilliant brush stroked of red down its chromed sides, or the subtle slash of red-orange under the jaw of a West Slope Cutthroat Trout, giving rise to its name; each uniquely designed by God himself.

I have had chills go up and down my spine at the sight and magnificent sound of a bull elk bugling his defiance at competitors for his cows in an open field. Perhaps you've stood at the blustery shores of the ocean or the edge of the Grand Canyon and marveled at the magnificence before you. Who among us hasn't gazed at the pink blossoms of a cherry tree in spring, or the brilliant umber colors of fall foliage and not thought, "Way to go, God!" And yet, and yet… these natural wonders were not God's finest. God wasn't yet finished creating.

Woman, you are the apex of natural wonders. You are the finest of all God's creation.

Beautiful woman reading this, don't ever forget that you have a divine mark, just like that on a piece of fine bone China. Whether pretty or plain, tall or short, you carry the brilliant DNA of Eve and the very image of God Himself (Gen. 1:27). You, like Eve, are fashioned by God Himself to birth new life, to nurture and care; you carry the capacity and capability to change the world for good.

> You, like Eve, are fashioned by God Himself to birth new life, to nurture and care; you carry the capacity and capability to change the world for good.

A Garden Wedding

Now for my favorite part of the story: after God made Eve, "… he brought her to the man" (Gen. 2:22). We are given an amazing glimpse into God's heart here and the first foreshadowing of Christ and His Bride, the Church, the hope of every Christian both single and married alike. Here God paints a picture that is reenacted in almost every outdoor Christian wedding today. I would like to believe that Adam and Eve's "wedding day" was utterly spectacular and memorable. God, after all, was the first wedding planner and had the ability to fashion a special day.

As a father, reading this passage in Genesis takes me back to an unforgettable day, the day that I gave my Carli away at her wedding. For me, the wedding day of my only daughter was fraught with mixed emotions for both of us…especially when the dad giving the bride away was also officiating the wedding like I was.

Carli and I have a special relationship, as only a father can truly understand. She alone can tug at my heartstrings like no one else. As she grew up and developed an engaging personality, she learned to approach me with a request by batting her gorgeous baby-blues and flipping her blond hair. "Daddy, join me for a tea party! Sure. "Daddy, do you have $20 I can borrow?" Of course. "Daddy, I'd like a horse"—that one took a few years, but in the end we had two horses pastured behind the house. "Yes, my dear Carli".

I was the first to hold this phenomenal tiny human being when she emerged from her mother's womb. I, too, changed her diapers, lifted her to my shoulders so she could see Shamu, pushed her higher in the swing, and tried to keep teenage boys at bay. In a very real sense, I helped shape and direct my lovely daughter's path. I am Dad. And now the ancient experience, debuted first by Eve against the most glorious backdrop of Eden, was about to be played out again, only this time with my baby girl. I couldn't stop the clock.

The day broke clear and calm after weeks of rain so this wedding could actually be held outside as planned, at the groom's family's ranch. On this fine June day, the white tents were set up on the green grass, the chairs were arranged perfectly and all the minute details were in place. By mid-day people began to arrive by the hundreds. All too soon it was "go time." There we were together one last time, father and daughter.

This was the last day that I would be the principal man in her life. Tomorrow she would wake up married.

As the bridesmaids and groomsmen made their way out of the house, we were left standing somewhat alone, together, Carli and me. We were intentionally avoiding looking at each other. Neither one of us is a crier. But we knew this moment was going to be paradoxically blessed and tough. I had been stealing glances at my daughter, as she stood in her stunning hand-picked wedding dress, face beautifully made up by her mother's skill with Mary Kay make-up, and her long professionally styled blond hair. I dared not look to long before my vision was blurred tears, long held back but ready to burst forth if I didn't man-up. Happy tears, yes, but tears of a father who was about to walk the aisle of change.

Old memories began to swirl through my mind that made my heart beat faster as the seconds ticked off the clock. I had thought about this day a thousand times throughout the years. The very first day that I stood over her crib, I began praying for her future husband. It was but the blink of an eye that I found myself twirling her five-year old self in a miniature wedding dress made by her grandma, they had all led into this special day.

As the bride's song began to play, it was our cue to head out the farmhouse door. Carli reached over and grabbed my left arm, which automatically elevated. I felt the sweet pressure of her delicate hand on my arm one last time. As we took our first steps towards the door, we stole a quick glance at each other... she biting her quivering lower lip and me... well, I don't really remember anything other than feeling the hot sting of tears welling up in my eyes... and we began the long march to the front of this Edenic outdoor sanctuary. Six hundred people rose in unison as we exited the house and watched the most ancient of ceremonies; a tear-streaked Father walking his daughter towards her soon to be husband. With a massive lump in my throat, I was about to give away my beloved "Poppy" to another, whose name interestingly enough is Adam.

I wonder if this how God felt when he escorted Eve to Adam? On God's arm, so to speak, was the loveliest creature, the future mother of all nations. Eve was the final brush stroke of His master piece. She was His precious girl, whose eyes had fluttered open wide when she gazed up into God's face, His was the first image she saw after He breathed new life into her lungs. No doubt God loved His Eve as Daddy and she adored her Maker as Father.

Right before God presented Eve to Adam, I wonder if He had any last minute concerns; "Would Adam love her? Would Adam accept her as a gift?" I'm pretty sure Adam's response answered any concerns the Lord might have had, for upon seeing Eve for the very first time, Adam said, "Wow, Baby, where have you been all my life?!"

I saw a similar response from my daughter's fiancé the morning of the wedding. In the monumental event called, "First Look," The groom, Adam, was standing in the yard with his back turned to the house. My daughter then silently slipped up behind him in full bridal regality and spoke his name. She whispered, "Adam". He turned, looked at his bride, my daughter, and was visibly wonderstruck, quietly undone by her beauty. Adam broke in to tears and they embraced. Those of stealing looks out the window sought out Kleenex boxes as well. The first man and woman looked into one another's eyes and in that sacred moment the first enterprise was born, the first matrimonial union, the finest model of co-leadership was established. Yes, in response to human need.

I like to imagine Adam's "first look" at Eve and the impact she had. Stunned, he saw in Eve someone just like him—"bone of my bones and flesh of my flesh"—yet different; "she shall be called 'woman,' for she was taken out of man" (Gen. 2:23). Biologically, they were almost identical, yet perfectly complimentary. Adam's reaction wasn't just, "She's one hot babe" kind-of-comment. Instead, it reflected a much bigger reality—he was no longer alone. Eve was designed by God to "fit him" to be his "help-mate." When they held one another in that first embrace, I wonder, did she touch his scar, knowing that her existence cost him something too?

I believe Scripture is clear that women have a special God-given role on earth to meet human need; penned into the very story of Eve is this simple, yet profound truth. Eve was formed second, not because she was an afterthought, but because she was desperately needed, which was God's original plan all along. Eve was specially designed by God to alleviate not only Adam's felt need, but she was God's answer to humanity's need. Adam saw God's divine reflection in Eve. Adam experienced God's goodness in Eve. Adam was drawn to Eve in a powerful way—as most men are still drawn to their "Eve" to this day. Genesis candidly describes it this way, "... a man leaves his father and mother and is united to his wife, and they become one flesh" (Gen. 2:24). This verse describes the attracting power of a woman who submits wholly to God's call on her life. When a woman finds her niche in life, complementary connections occur that are nothing short of divine—connections with power that can move mountains. Women were designed to be world changers in a way completely unique; women are God's indescribable gift to us. When a woman finds a need that she has been designed to fill, something extraordinary happens. Partnerships are formed. Lives are changed. The world they live in becomes a better place. Thus was the case with Mary Kay Ash, a woman who founded the company that still bears her name. I want to share her story because she, Mary Kay, made a profound impact on my life through my wife, Disa's, involvement with the company for over 30 years. Disa was personally trained and encouraged by Mary Kay and brought her "can do" spirit into our home.

One Woman Can

The 1950-60's were brutal for women in America's workforce. The glass ceiling, as we know it, was more likely a steel ceiling. In many settings, men were paid twice as much as women for the same type of work. There was a significant need for a company that would allow women the freedom and opportunity to prosper. The seeds for that kind of company were being planted in the 40's and 50's when a divorced mother of three worked her way up the ladder of success in a direct sales company called Stanley Home Products.

This industrious woman needed the flexibility of direct sales so she could still be involved in her children's lives. She worked hard and often exceeded the sales quotas for the month while competing head-to-head with men. After several years of success, she was promoted to the position of National Sales Director but being a woman, she was blocked from the management position, and was paid half as much as other men in the same job. More than once she had been asked by the company to train a man, who was later promoted to be her superior. Here was a hard-working, talented female whose head was pressed up against the proverbial glass ceiling.

After 25 years with this company she retired, frustrated and somewhat embittered. While the company had provided her with a decent means to support her family, it always treated her as a second-class citizen. In her retirement she set out to write a book. A book that would help women learn from her two decades of experience in a male-dominated career track. So she wrote down all the life lessons she learned, hoping to draft a management-training program. Instead it planted the seed of a dream. More specifically, these notes led her to outline a business plan for her "dream company."

On Friday, September 13, 1963, Mary Kay Cosmetics was founded. 50-plus years later, Mary Kay lands at #141 on the Forbes list of America's Largest Private companies.[3] With an independent sales force of over 2 million people—mostly women—who sold over 4 billion dollars of product in 2015, Mary Kay products are sold in more than 35 markets around the world. There are over 5,000 employees who support this massive sales force.[4] Mary Kay's dream came true in a big way. Many of the women who rose to the top have literally earned millions of dollars in their careers along with lavish international trips, prizes and cars—including the famous Mary Kay Pink Cadillac. It is accurate to say that there are no glass ceilings in Mary Kay, Inc.[5]

Mary Kay Ash was, and still is, "Eve" to hundreds of thousands of women. By that I mean she was uniquely shaped and led by God to meet a pressing human need. Founding the company that still bears her name was her God-given purpose in life. Many of those within the company revere her still. My wife, who has been involved with the company for over 33 years, was one of the last groups of Directors that were personally trained by Mary Kay herself. And I am one of the few "Mary Kay husbands" who say that they actually talked to this remarkable woman in person.[6]

Think about the women in history who broke through their male-dominated cultures to rise to their divine mission. Think of the many more whose potential is staggering. Why do you think the serpent tempted Eve first? *I am certain it was because Eve was the linchpin upon which history would hang.* Maybe the serpent knew something that we have overlooked in Genesis… Eve's potential and ability to complete things at a deep level for good, giving glory to God.

Enemy in a Perfect Setting

Even in the perfect setting, Eve had an enemy. The serpent was later identified as Satan. To this very day, all women, the descendants of Eve, still have the same enemy: Satan. In one sense Satan's attacks have not changed, he still wants you—modern day Eves—to doubt God's heart. You see, the first Eve was made to believe that God was holding out on her. She was tricked into believing that her Creator was no longer trustworthy. She forgot her purpose. She forgot her role. She thought that she needed, and maybe even deserved, "more." Instead of seeing herself as the divine solution to humanity's need, she wanted to see herself as the keeper of what is right and wrong (i.e. knowing good and evil), a position of power reserved only for God. There are a thousand ways that the original lie is played out in the lives of women today.

Still, history is replete with women, in various cultures, who have risen to meet a great need and changed the world by their leadership. Whether the task be large or small, at home, in a village, in a sky rise, or on a huge piece of machinery, "woman" is especially designed to birth new beginnings and change lives.

In 1861 the first units of federal troops poured into Washington, D.C. Hungry, ill-equipped and wounded they presented a terrific need in the early stages of the Civil war. Clara Barton was working as a recording clerk in the U.S. Patent Office in Washington, D.C. and saw the need. This teacher turned clerk launched a movement to help these soldiers in the upcoming bloodiest war in American History. She was later to be known as the "Angel of the Battlefield" for her valiant efforts to provide supplies for front line surgeons. On May 21, 1881, Clara Barton was instrumental in founding the American Red Cross.[7]

September 5, 1980, MADD was incorporated. Mothers Against Drunk Driving or MADD. This powerful organization was birthed out of the anguish of a mom. Candice (Candy) Lightner, who is noted as the organizer and the founding president of MADD, channeled her grief into solving a massive problem. On May 3, 1980, Lightner's 13-year-old daughter, Cari, was killed in a hit-and-run accident. The 46 year old drunk driver, who had recently been arrested for another DUI hit-and-run, left Cari's body at the scene. Lightner got mad. She saw a problem and created a movement that continues on to this day. MADD has successfully changed public opinion and national policy and laws regarding drinking and driving. One woman can make a profound difference; it is her Eve-like design.

Google "Women who changed the world" and you'll find all kinds of listings of women who have made a difference for good (sure, there are some who did not bring about positive changes). I believe that all women have Eve's ability to change the world they live in for good. Maybe it's as simple as caring for a neighbor's child, or taking a meal to an elderly shut-in that has been forgotten, or starting a dream company.

> All women have Eve's ability to change the world they live in for good.

As a vocational pastor, my church would utterly shut down if all the women who volunteer quit at the same time. From cradle to grave, I have teams of women making a difference in the lives of my people and thereby impacting our community. Shirley has led Bingo at a nursing home for years. Shari volunteers hundreds of hours a year at a local benevolence agency. Both are widows who chose not to stay home but get out and make a difference.

Heather, half East Indian ("dot-not-feather" as she says) and half Caucasian, is a world-changer. She travels the treacherous back roads of India, Nepal, Thailand and other Asian countries, visiting orphanages and recruiting orphans and at-risk children to sing in the Matsiko World Orphan Choir[8] which raises funds for these forgotten ones so they can be fed and educated. I know she gets discouraged at how big a mess our world is in, but I keep encouraging her to make a difference wherever and however she can. She is Eve to hundreds of kids, giving them hope in hopeless settings.

We must remember, however, that women are still under attack from the Devil himself. In May of 2014, over three hundred Nigerian girls—mostly Christian—were kidnapped by an Islamic terrorist group called *Boko Haram*, led by Abubakar Shekau, because they wanted an education. *Boko Haram* means, "Western Education is Forbidden." These girls face a dire future if intervention isn't timely. Only two girls have been returned[9] to their families leaving the fate of the others yet to be determined.

Thousands of young girls (and sometimes boys as well) from around the world are forced into the sex trades. While a vicious human condition, it is still nothing other than an all-out attack against women. Pornography, in all its media forms, is demeaning and degrading to all women, portraying them as objects of desire rather than, the world-class problem solvers and partners they were designed to be. While I write about these atrocities, I wonder, in light of Eve's design, when men will lock arms with our women for change. When will we fall into step with those, who in their fullest femininity and power, lead the charge against the needs in humanity? What more shall I say? "Women", I say, "Rise up and change this crazy world"! Your world. My world. God's world. Your passion to make a difference is hard wired into every cell of your body by design. Write your book. Run for office. Travel the world, bringing hope to the hopeless. Hug your baby and raise a generation to trust God for the impossible.

Questions For Discussion

1. What take a ways do you have from the discussion about Eve before the Fall? After her fall?

2. How have you viewed women's roles on earth—as problem solvers—prior to reading this chapter?

3. What are some of the lies that you've believed about yourself?

4. If money or social position were no problem, what would you do to change the world?

5. What dream seed has God placed in your heart?

6. What are you going to do about it?

Chapter Three

Job's Grief

Taking Life On Life's Terms

Naked I came from my mother's womb, and naked I will depart.
The Lord gave and the Lord has taken away; may the name of
the Lord be praised.

Job 1:21

A child dies. A father is taken too soon by a drunk driver. A son is killed in
Afghanistan by a roadside bomb. These kinds of graveside services are a gut
check for the depth of our faith. In my role as pastor, I am there all too often.
Some of us walk away from the casket in utter despair, not knowing what

to do next. What would happen if we understood the ancient rhythm of life and death? Is it possible to recover from the valley of grief? Many of us have experienced significant loss; yet few know how to step through the minefields of grief. Here, formulaic myths often associated with love and loss will be dispelled, guiding you to a deeper understanding of God's role in loss. This chapter may raise a few more questions than it answers. The truth is that there are some things about God and life that will always remain a mystery. Letting go of our demand for answers is not only helpful, but healthy.

I knew it was going to be a hard day. My wife and I were driving to Greeley, Colorado on a mission…to visit my brother's grave. Kent and I were born just eleven months apart, he being the older. Growing up, we were often mistaken for twins. We shared friends, adventures and faith, and our older brother, Kevin and little sister Sue Anne. There were three boys just three years apart, four children in all six years apart; yes, our poor mother!

Our early years were chock full of bicycles, baseball, and outdoor adventures, but after high school Kent and I drifted far apart. The decades slid past like the steady current of water flowing down the Platte River where we grew up. Across the years there were a few visits and an occasional Christmas card, but little else. No new stories were birthed from shared adventures as adults; chapters forever left unwritten.

I had last seen Kent lying in a hospital bed in the early spring of 2010. Years in the sun had produced the most dangerous type of skin cancer—melanoma—that had metastasized and invaded Kent's body, eventually reaching his brain. Knowing that his condition was terminal, I'd flown out to Greeley that year. He was on the short list, so to speak, and we needed to talk. How does one begin to say what hadn't been said for over 30 years? How many minutes or hours would it take to cover enough ground to begin the overdue conversation about life and death?

When I first laid eyes on my middle brother lying in the sterile environment of the hospital, a wave of emotions surged, taking a herculean effort to push back. This visit wasn't about me. It was about him. It was about us. It was about hope. My grief had to wait.

After trudging through a few difficult days of pushing Kent around in a wheelchair while he received radiation treatments, the Lord provided us with one special moment. At last, two lost brothers' hearts touched once again. I had wheeled Kent outside to catch a little fresh air. We were both born for the outdoors and needed space. While he looked off into the distance, I began to share with him words of hope and regret that had been bottled up for years. At first the words came slowly, but soon they found a rhythm and I asked to share a story from Scripture.

My brother had accepted Christ as a youth. I was there that day, so long ago, at church camp, located in the rolling Sandhills of north central Nebraska, where he professed his faith and was baptized in Pible Lake. Soon after high school, though, he followed a darker path…getting his teen-age girlfriend pregnant and marrying into a deeply dysfunctional family that led him away from the church. In contrast, I became ever more involved in the church, accepting a call to vocational ministry and earning several college degrees along the way. We not only drifted apart economically, educationally and emotionally, but I also lost track of my brother. There were several years where I didn't know where Kent was or what he was doing. All I knew was that he had abandoned his first family and always seemed on the run.

Now, many years later, we found ourselves awkwardly sitting together on unfamiliar hospital ground, the clock ticking. I retold the story of the Prodigal Son from the Gospel of Luke, Chapter 15. I said that it was *our story*—two brothers in need of their Father's embrace. My motive was pure. I desperately wanted Kent to know that God loved him and was willing and able to welcome him back if he would just turn toward home.

With the pain of all those lost years choking my voice and tears welling up in my eyes, I did my best to throw him a lifeline. Years of practiced speaking and advanced degrees were useless as I looked into his weathered face. I didn't know if he heard a thing because he kept looking away. I finally pushed my own doubts aside and whispered, "Kent, I came here to show you that I love you and that God loves you and I want to see you in heaven after you die."

After a long pause with the spring wind ruffling his unkempt hair, he turned his leathery face towards me and I looked into his brown eyes—eyes that often filled with despondency and shame. This time they were different. In that moment I got a glimpse of my brother's soul. Kent had heard God's word. The story of the Prodigal touched him deeply. Locked eye-to-eye, he simply said, "Don't worry little brother, I'll be there."

Even now as I pen these words, I weep. "I'll be there." Somehow I know it's true. God's word ignited the tiny flame of faith that Kent had held on to all those years and even while he sat in that wheelchair, he once again turned his feet toward home. He'll be there. He is already there, waiting and watching for me. The Prodigal will be welcoming his little brother into the party!

. . . .

I held on to that recent memory as I walked into the Lin Grove Cemetery of Greeley months later on a cool September afternoon. My wife knew that this was a stop I needed to make alone. She dropped me off and pulled away from the curb. I stood for a while trying to get my bearings. I could hear the traffic passing by on nearby Highway 34. Birds were chirping and somewhere someone was mowing their grass. The cemetery was a typical well-manicured lawn with granite tombstones marking the graves of others who had passed away. I could smell the earthiness of this place of final rest. And I was alone. For a moment or two my feet felt like they were stuck in concrete blocks, not wanting to move forward. Part of me wanted to be there; the other part wanted to run. Regretfully, I had not gone back for Kent's memorial service held in April, at a church that he had never attended. This was my own private memorial, my chance to say good-bye.

In my hands I held a cemetery map, trying to find Kent's unmarked grave—located in the section of the cemetery where the state buries the poor. Using the map as a guide, I walked east and stopped several times, searching the grounds, row-by-row, looking for Kent's grave. Pausing underneath the shade of a mountain ash tree, I looked down to see a newly dug grave. Could it be his? I looked closer at the sunken sod and saw a simple wooden cross. It had been placed at the head of the grave but had since fallen over. I picked it up and held it in my hands. In simple letters was written, "Kent David Nelson," my brother. Here it was at last, Kent's final resting place.

My vision blurred. Time stopped. I stood there taking in the story that this grave told, "Here lies a man that only a few knew, and fewer still loved." Then I could stand no longer. The weight of the lost years, the missed opportunities and the utter brokenness of our relationship crushed me to the ground. My breathing was staggered and laborious as I surrendered to the repressed pain of regret that could no longer be denied.

Grief surged in waves like an ocean shoreline in winter, revealing the effects of storms far removed, yet altogether real. I dug my fingers deep into the broken sod. I wet the ground with snot and tears long held back. I gave voice to words that had lain dormant for too long. I whispered, "Kent I loved you so much, and I missed you! I wanted to fish and hunt and hang out with you! Where were you? What happened to you? Why did you choose to go away, so far away?" Then the deeper stuff surged forth as I told him, "I am so sorry that I didn't come looking when you got lost. Please forgive me. I'm so sorry that I judged you and broke off contact. Oh Jesus, I'm so sorry!"

Time surged ahead and the grief began to dissipate. I said my piece. Before I left, I reached deep into my jeans pocket and retrieved a small, smooth basalt rock, about an inch in diameter. I had found an identical pair of these black beauties on the sandy shores of Cannon Beach, Oregon that previous winter. I liked how they fit in the palm of my hand. I had taken them with me to Greeley and had given Kent one when he was in the hospital. I kept the other one. When he inquired about the small black stone, I said, "When things get tough in the next few weeks, hold that stone in your hand and remember that Jesus is your rock and remember that you have a brother who loves you."

When visiting his grave site, I took a different rock picked up for this occasion, pulled up some loose sod on his grave and pushed it into the soft earth. I can't really remember what I said, but it was something like, "I'll see you soon." The other smooth black stone still sits on the windowsill of my home office reminding me of Kent's promise and my future. I will hold on to this experience when my final days draw near, trusting in God for a future with my middle brother.

Unpacking the Story of Job

I share this personal story with you as a lead into a discussion about life's harsh realities. We've all lost something of importance or someone dear. It is the human condition. Whether it's the untimely death of a loved one, a loss of health, or a job failure, the journey of loss always includes three movements. Like a great orchestral piece, it is powerful and somewhat predictable. Yet, the whispering truths of the book of Job are usually shouted down by the false ideas and theologies that well-meaning churchgoers have picked up along the way. Let me be clear: I don't have a hyped up formula to get you through life's interruptions. There is no formula. You might want to read that again. Anyone who claims to offer such a remedy for life's breakdowns and mishaps is selling snake oil.

One of the common problems I discovered in life, is that we all want a quick three-step process to resolve the challenges brought about by disruption. We want a "spiritual prescription" for what ails us. Seriously, as a pastor who has counseled hundreds, many come to me hoping for a quick and painless spiritually-directed solution. But when I suggest that they might consider being "fully present" in their pain to find God's presence in it—that they are literally being shaped by God in the disruption—few make a follow-up visit. Instead, some ask for a referral to a local counselor, hoping to find someone who can help them figure things out in a shorter time frame. At the risk of sounding harsh, I can say that many people have sat in my office or out on the lake, and declared that "life shouldn't be so hard." To which I often want to ask (but rarely do), "Really? Who said? Didn't Jesus say, "In this world you will have trouble" (Jn. 16:33)?

Even I have preached sermons offering quick, prescription outlines until I realized I was perpetuating a myth. Prescriptive Christianity doesn't work. When we are brutalized by the waves of a personal tsunami, we rarely have time to come up for air, let alone apply some prepackaged ideas about God and life to alleviate the suffering sustained by the situation. In contrast, what most of us are looking for in the storm surge is a lifeline, something to hang onto while the waves crash against us, hoping that we won't drown. To borrow a phrase from my AA friends, Job is a book that teaches us to "accept life completely on life's terms."[10]

The Rhythm of Job

My personal story of grief and restoration was shared as a segue into a discussion of one of the oldest, most interesting, and mysterious books of the Bible—Job. To wrestle with the meaning and purposes of disruption requires me to talk briefly about the book and particularly about the person himself. After all, Job is not merely a crafted theology of suffering (or disruption), although one could argue that, but rather a story. Job is a true story of a real man whose world was torn apart by interruption.

Let me state clearly that this short chapter is in no way a complete commentary on this most ancient of biblical texts. I'll leave that to scholars. Speaking from my perspective only, many have tried to describe the book of Job as something it's not—a tidy little book of answers to the questions posed by human suffering. Job often leaves a reader asking more questions than it answers. One huge meta-principle I believe that the book puts forth is this: A relationship with God through faith is a demanding way of life that rarely offers a ready fix for our problems.

Old Testament scholar Walter Brueggemann suggests that the story of Job follows a pattern, which he describes as *orientation, disorientation*, and *new orientation*.[11] Borrowing from Brueggemann the remainder of this chapter will explain the three-part movement of disruption utilizing the key word "reality" in place of "orientation." I describe the journey of spiritual formation through interruption as set forth in the book of Job as consisting of three key movements: 1) A present reality, 2) A disrupted reality and 3) A new reality. I have found this "trilogy of disruption" helpful both personally and professionally while guiding those who are caught in the fog of the "in between." I call these three realities "movements" because life isn't filled with clearly delineated sign posts indicating spiritual growth, but rather re-directions that are strung together like a couple of nice turns in downhill skiing.

A Present Reality

A present reality describes the "right now" or the "present moment." In Job's case, just a few verses describe the reality of his life, *before disruption* (Job 1:1-2:13). In these lines we see that Job's life was rich and full by any measure. The Bible describes him as "…the greatest man among all the people of the East" (Job 1:3). He had it all: fame, fortune and family. You could say that the Lord had backed up the "Good Life" truck and dumped it in his lap. He was the man others would point at and say, "I want to be like Job." But his fortune didn't last long.

In a conversation with God, Satan accused Job of only loving God because of the blessing poured out on his life, suggesting that if the blessing went away so would Job's faith. In a drama that still leaves theologians scratching their heads, God granted Satan permission to interrupt Job's life with one condition—Satan couldn't kill Job. This Scripture can kick the day-lights out of someone's neat and tidy view of God. Job is good at that.

The implications of this ancient story are absolutely mind-boggling and beyond reason, even for seasoned Bible scholars. This most ancient of books leaves us all breathless to think that God allowed Satan to crush his beloved Job. The purpose of this chapter is not to explore all the theological implications of God's sovereignty, but rather to look at the realism portrayed in this man's experience with interruption. Let me say this clearly: *God can redeem any and all disruptions in our lives, whatever the cause. Whether it is from God, from Satan, from humankind or nature, all can be re-shaped by our Creator for our good and that of the world we live in.*

A Disrupted Reality

A disrupted reality is clearly displayed through Job's story. It is hard to find the words to describe what happens next. Mildly stated, Job's life was interrupted and thrown into complete disorientation. His life went from predictable to absolutely crazy. His world was rocked to the core. Satan tore Job's life apart piece by piece, a wolf ripping at fallen prey. First he destroyed Job's immense wealth and livelihood via raiders and natural disaster (fire). As if that weren't enough, Satan somehow killed all of Job's children, and later inflicted God's favorite guy with a debilitating disease, all in that order (Job 1:12-19; 2:7).

How did Job respond to these massive events without cracking up? Scripture says "Job stood up and tore his robe in grief. Then he shaved his head and fell to the ground..." (Job 1:20). No surprise here. Wouldn't you pile up in a heap if someone told you all your children were dead—let alone that you lost your livelihood to thieves and acquired a chronic disease?

The Biblical text here is interesting. It doesn't just say that Job fell to the ground, but that he fell to the ground *with purpose*. Interestingly, Job "... fell to the ground to worship" (Job 1:20). This was no ordinary church service. This was not some small group meeting where God's man shed a tear or two as he told his story. This was a moment frozen in time where Job was overwhelmed by great loss, but not ruined. He chose to embrace the pain and grieve. He chose to feel the magnitude of the moment. The only way he could demonstrate the tearing of his soul was to rend his clothes and shave his head—signs of shame and brokenness. He was broken-hearted and alone. I can so relate. Job's reaction to the weight of grief reminds me of my graveside experience for my beloved brother. There are moments in time where words are replaced by the unintelligible sounds of grief.

Job was married. But his wife did not understand nor did she enter into her husband's suffering. It is evident her faith was wavering, or completely washed out, when she counseled her husband to, "Curse God and die" (Job 2:9). He was alone in a way that only those with alienated relationships know.

Still, Job worshiped. He honored God in the midst of misery. He decided then and there not to abandon his faith. He surprised Satan with a faith tempered like a fine Toledo steel sword of ancient times. Job's faith, as we see from the rest of the book, was the real deal. It wasn't built on God's material blessings alone, but on the character and nature of God; a God who reserves the right to give and to take away.

One of the temptations of trying to discern the theology of Job is to forget about his humanness. We catch a glimpse of Job's soul-ache caused by these horrendous events when he says, "Naked I came from my mother's womb, and naked I will depart. The Lord gave and the Lord has taken away; may the name of the Lord be praised" (Job 1:20-21). These tragedies shook him to his core. They blew his world apart. All he had known, his blessings—his prosperity, his family, his prestige—was ripped from his grasp. Yet, the book of Job points out something amazing: "In all this, Job did not sin by charging God with wrongdoing" (Job 1:22). Job kept his faith. And through his life we can see a common journey that we, too, can choose when life gets interrupted.

Interruptions are disorienting each and every time. We can lose our bearing when a rogue wave of life hits our tidy ship. Like passengers who experienced the Poseidon adventure, sometimes our whole world gets turned upside down by events that are completely outside of our control. Could it be that this is part of the design; part of God's plan to shape us spiritually? When are we most likely to ask for direction? When we're lost or when we think we know the way? When are we most likely to seek the Lord's help? When life is good and there's food in the cupboard, a nice car parked in the driveway, or when the Great Recession strips us bare?

Satan erroneously believed that Job's faith was only based on his material blessings. Scripture goes to great lengths to remind us that Job held tightly to his faith in contrast to the things of life that he seemingly held loosely. Even in the midst of the chaos Job credits God for both blessing and

> **Even in the midst of the chaos Job credits God for both blessing and curse.**

curse (Job 1:20). Job was a realist. He understood clearly that we leave this world exactly how we entered it, empty-handed. Therefore, it seems according to this ancient entrepreneur, that anything we get between birth and death is simply a bonus.

Job's friends show up in the midst of his disruption (don't' miss the timing of this) to offer advice. Advice that is later revealed to be offensive to God (Job 42:7) Even Job's reasoning is challenged when God says to him, "Who is this that obscures my plans with words without knowledge. Brace yourself like a man; I will question you, and you shall answer me" (Job 38:2-3).

What follows is the longest monologue of God in Scripture. It came as a response to man's incessant demand for answers to the questions that arise from the quagmire of disruption. What was God's recorded answer to the questions birthed from Job's life quake? *There weren't any.* Instead of answering, God asks more questions. (i.e. "Where were you when I laid the earth's foundation?"). What can we take away from this? *Maybe answers aren't always the answer.*

A New Reality

Fortunately for us, God didn't leave Job in ashes, but instead guided him to a new reality. Let's skip to the end of this ancient story as recorded in Job 43:12. "The Lord blessed the latter part of Job's life more than the former part." God restored his faithful follower. God gave Job more than he had before. Still, things would never be what they once were. They couldn't be. There is no question in my mind that there wasn't a day that would go by that Job didn't think about and grieve his first family. Maybe like me, he went to the site where they were tragically killed and grieved the loss.

Things were different for Job now. Not better or worse. *Just different.* A new reality. His faith was still intact after all the craziness. God had been vindicated and the Accuser was silenced as he witnessed a man of faith, a man who still believed when he had nothing; when life had fallen apart.

The degree to which we understand this tri-fold pattern of life will determine our happiness with our new reality after disruption. Everything changes. This doesn't mean that I no longer wish for what was, but that I can come to a place of accepting my new reality. I don't even have to like it. It is interesting that this acceptance often results in a sense of peace emanating from a stronger and deeper faith.

Is this a one-time experience? No. Will we continue to be invited to move to new realities out of disruption for the remainder of our lives? Yes. Unequivocally yes. Why should we be treated differently than Job?

. . . .

After my visit to Kent's gravesite, Disa and I drove out to I-80 East, towards my childhood home town of Cozad, Nebraska. The weather set the mood for the occasion—grey and raining. Disa drove me to all the places where my brothers and I had built great memories decades before as kids I directed her to the empty lots, parks, and school grounds where we played pick-up games of baseball, basketball and football. Places that the "three musketeers:" Kevin the eldest, Kent the middle child, and Tony the little tag-along-brother, laughed and cried, fought and lived.

As mentioned earlier, my brothers and I also had a little sister, Sue Anne, who was also a big part of our growing up years. Sue was the last born and had to navigate life dealing with three older brothers—no small feat! She was the tender and compassionate one; adopting stray dogs and making friends with the friendless. She was deeply wounded by Kent's untimely passing and distant life. In many ways this chapter is written for those of us who remain. I am hoping and praying that others might find comfort and healing in the Savior who helped me pen these words.

A deep healing happened for me on that trip. To be totally honest, I don't know how it happened. But I do know Who the healer is: Jesus, the Christ. It was Jesus who walked with me into the cemetery. It was Jesus who stood by my side as I visited my hometown and relived childhood memories, both good and bad. It was Jesus, a "Man of Sorrows" (Isa. 53:3a), who was there beside me, weeping with me, laughing and remembering. It made all the difference in the world, for He, too, is my brother.

I continue to relate to the Scripture that reminds me to grieve with hope (1 Thess. 4:13). I again feel the sting of grief as I write this chapter, but it's different. I feel more hope than loss. By supernatural grace, I've been released from decades of disappointment. While I will always remember my loss, I have let go of the whip handle of regret and now forgive myself and treat these memories with greater kindness. In the time since, I have stopped blaming God and let Him off the hook as well, learning a little more each day to take life on life's terms.

May our epitaph be that of Job who died ...*an old man and full of years* (Job 42:17).

Questions for Discussion

1. Have you had a "Job" experience? Describe personal tsunamis that rocked your world.
2. How did this disruption impact your faith?
3. Do you demand answers?
4. Do you find it difficult to embrace the people in your present because you are longing for something or someone from the past?
5. How could a better understanding of the "trilogy of life"— present reality, disrupted reality, new reality—help you or others navigate through life's disruptions?

Chapter Four

Abraham's Flexibility
Understanding Life As A Journey

The Lord had said to Abram, "Go from your country, your people and your father's household to the land I will show you..."
Genesis 12:1

Is life a journey or a destination? Your answer could ultimately determine your happiness and personal growth as a human being. If life is a destination, we have little reason to believe that our purpose is more than protecting and maintaining our "space;" creating a defensive approach to most of life. If life is a journey, then we can embrace the constant challenges that bring change and experience significant growth as a result. Protecting our space leaves little room for creative thinking; while looking at life as journey creates an attitude of abundance and curiosity. In this chapter we will step into the biblical story of the great Patriarch Abraham, one whose life portrays the value of journey and an attitude of flexibility. We will see Abraham's deepening relationship with God in the midst of life's unforeseen and agonizing challenges, as well as his character defects and failures, reminding us that perfection is not congruent with life as journey. We still talk and write about Abraham and Sarah thousands of years later because their flexibility and journey of faith created a legacy for us.

Today I'm sitting in a borrowed house. It's a big, beautiful house—over 4,000 square feet of "amazing"—massive hand hewn supporting timbers, custom wood floors, fancy fixtures, granite counter tops and sinks, two indoor fire places, massive rooms and an amazing view of Lake Coeur d'Alene (Idaho), just begins to describe its beauty. Dear friends of ours offered Disa and I a chance to housesit for them while they winter in sunny Arizona. We are astounded and blessed with their generosity. This is not a honeymoon get-away for us, however.

Their housesitting offer came at just the right time, in the midst of a *major* life disruption. I had just resigned from a 22-year ministry in the small North Idaho town of Sandpoint. It came as a negotiated result after several years of conflict with the elder board. To say that our exit was harmonious would be far from accurate. My wife and I did our best to exit as peacefully as we could, for the sake of the church, but our hearts were torn apart when asked to leave by the elders. I did not resign to take another ministry; I resigned under pressure with no job in place. It felt like a huge injustice. Yes, it was ultimately my decision. Disa and I believed at the time that it was what was best for both our beloved church and for me as their leader. The stress of the conflict was tearing me down mentally, physically and emotionally.

Three weeks after announcing my resignation, I walked away from my work, my wonderful staff, my church family, local pastors, and long-time friendships. The relational cost was devastating, especially to my wife, who had developed some very loving relationships over 22 years with several generations of our church family. One of the highlights of my wife's typical week was greeting the children who sought her out each and every Sunday for a piece of gum and a hug. She was the "Pied Piper" of our gathering. Disa searched out young parents, giving their arms a much-needed break by offering to hold their newborns. Holding and loving babies brings her such joy. Along with almost every other cadence in her life, this rhythm was torn from her grasp with little warning.

This was *not* how we had envisioned our ministry coming to an end in Sandpoint—under so much duress. We have come to describe my resignation as an unwanted divorce. The details that led up to this departure are not as important as the end result where we, like the ancient patriarchs of our Christian faith—Abraham and Sarah—we found ourselves leaving everything that was familiar, for an uncertain future.

I share this deeply personal story to prove a point: *disruption is difficult.* Let me rephrase that—*disruption can be downright overwhelming.* Life interruptions, whether good or bad, are unsettling and can lead to despair and a crisis of faith. By a crisis of faith, I mean a person can wake up in the midst of a traumatic transition and wonder, "God, where were you? Why did this happen now? Is this really what you want? Really?" At the center of this interrogation—"God, why didn't you do something to stop this madness from happening?!"

Perhaps you can relate. Maybe you, too, lost a job unjustly. After we left this ministry, I felt like a used up toy that had been tossed away. In the midst of that pain, several well meaning people and close friends, said things like: "We know that God has something better for you in the future." While I appreciated their cheerful motive, it made me wonder,

"What about right now?" We hear that phrase enough to realize that it is one of those things we say when we don't know how else to express care for those who are hurting. But is it true? Does God have something better for us in the future? Was it God's plan to allow such upheaval in our lives? If so, to what end?

My wife and I are not totally through our story; in fact, we're just barely on the front end of a new adventure. I share this personal account with you on the likely chance that you may have picked up this book and turned to this chapter to find some direction in the midst of your own life-disruption. Maybe your spouse just filed for divorce, or your company restructured and you were let go. Maybe you got angry and walked out with no plan. You are a person of faith and now, like us, your faith is undergoing a test and the results are yet to be determined. Will you pass or will you fail? Will your reliance on God be stronger down the road or merely a distant memory?

These kinds of questions really can't be answered with anecdotal comments or fairy tale theology. Instead, we need to go to Scripture. Disruptions, especially the big ones that stop us in our tracks, usually bring with them some level of spiritual crisis, even when they are self-imposed or when we are following hard after the Lord. What does the Bible say about life as journey? We can study God's story and find people who experienced similar things as most of us do, just in a different time. I am always amazed to find in the pages of God's Word timeless principles that transfer across the centuries and apply to our very personal circumstances.

Abraham is called the Father of Our Faith, so I figured he was a good one to enlist for a lesson about what lies ahead, starting with my own uncertain future. I don't hold the answers on this, but rather am embarking with deep vulnerability. Let's turn to Abraham's story to discover some wisdom and the Spirit's nudge while navigating through life's unforeseen events.

When I look at my current personal situation, I'm humbled to realize that our disruption is quite minimal when compared to Abraham's. God wasn't asking Abraham to take a little side road or detour; God's invitation to journey was going to be a steep climb. Abraham and Sarah were being asked to move over 500 miles to a new land on foot (or a rough riding cart). Abraham and his father Terah had already moved 600 miles along the Fertile Crescent from Ur of Chaldea to Tehran. There they settled and seemingly became prosperous, acquiring land, livestock and servants. At age 75, when most people would have been preparing a burial plot, God asked an old man to chase a dream. What was the dream? The dream was to become a nation, through an son, that would ultimately bless the entire world, by another Son.

> At age 75, when most people would have been preparing a burial plot, God asked an old man to chase a dream.

The Keys to Moving Through Life's Disruptions

It is my hope that the following outline will help each of us sail through the rough seas of change. The acronym is simple, but it addresses a very complex challenge that almost all of us must face. Disa and I have re-discovered the truth in that little cliché about life not being a destination, but a journey. I know you've heard it, but have you embraced it for all its messiness and beauty and character-forming ability? I must admit, there have been moments when the prospect of striking out on the path of the unknown once again, excites me. The Lord has already shown Himself faithful to us. The gorgeous estate we were entrusted to housesit was an abundant gift. Getting time to finish this book was an unforeseen blessing. Like many of you, we're just putting one foot in front of the other as we follow the Lord's lead, being like Abraham, not really knowing where we're going.

J.O.U.R.N.E.Y.

J is for Journey

You probably have a plaque hanging on your wall stating, "Life is a journey," yet too many of us pitch a tent and turn it into a granite temple. We do good things, sinking roots and build relationships, thinking that these places, this job, those friendships will never change. But they can, and they will. My wife and I are still reeling emotionally. This means, it is quite possible that we had built a temple in our minds about my previous ministry, home and relationships.

In three months, we emptied out our home of over 20 years, sorted through our belongings, decided what to put in storage, and what we'd move with us. We moved 70 miles away to live in this gorgeous borrowed home, knowing that in just a few months we'll have to move it all again, and then probably again in another year. This is not fun. In our early years, we embraced mobility like this, when it seemed par for the course. At this present stage in our lives, "devastated," "heart-broken," "overwhelmed" and "depressed" are just a few of the words that describe us on any given day. You may be nodding your head and thinking, "Yeah, but you should hear my story." I get it. For years I was the pastor who counseled people through change, now I am on the other side of the desk seeking advice. Humbling? You bet. Terrifying? Absolutely.

My wife and I are now living in the "in-between." For us, this time is when we're in-between jobs, houses, and relationships. Abraham and Sarah lived the remainder of their lives, after leaving their home-land, in the land of, "in-between." Called by God to be life-long nomads, their lives would become ones of moving from one tent site to another, traveling the entire distance of the Fertile Crescent. As I reflected on their *call of mobility*, I began to wonder, "Could it be that we are the most open to and in need of the Lord's presence and provision in these "in-between time?; the times of aching ambiguity?" Abraham had some of his greatest experiences with God during his travels. They inspired him to keep pressing on—seven God-encounters in all.[12] Seven. Not seventy. Just seven. Just enough divine encounters or "God winks" (as our dear friend Jan Harris likes to say), to keep Abraham putting one foot in front of the other.

Much like our forefathers and mothers in ancient days, we find a lot of stops along the way. Some stops take longer than they should, perhaps, but the fact remains: we're always leaving some older place and moving toward something new. God keeps prodding us along to keep us from becoming too self-dependent on our own successes and abilities. Otherwise, we might settle for a life that is less than God intended.

God is training us now for a possible future adventure. Disa and I are on the front end of a new faith walk—*or crawl*—as God pulls us away from a familiar life we held onto so tightly for 22 years. If we're willing to let go of what we "know" for the "unknown", like Abraham and Sarah, we can welcome change in its many forms. For some of us, preparation feels like climbing a steep hill today without knowing why. I've done enough back-country hiking to know that I am much better off if my legs are toughened up before the demand to carry a heavy pack is thrust upon me. It is miserable to attempt steep trails when I'm not in shape. When our legs, our very lives, toughen up, we're able to conquer whatever the trail throws at us and reach the mountaintop.

O is for Overcome.

I don't think the old saying, "What doesn't kill you makes you stronger" is true for everyone, because sometimes "What doesn't kill you just makes you grouchy and bitter!" This life principle is clear... hardship can push us to become a better person by finding meaning and purpose in our trials. We can find a deeper friendship with Jesus along the way, or, we can choose to be embittered.

Abraham and Sarah had to overcome a litany of challenges: financial, relational (Abraham and nephew, Lot, got into a big family feud and parted ways), and vocational. They had to overcome their sin (Abram's lying got them in hot water numerous times), they had to overcome their fears and their impatience (can you say Ishmael—Abrahams illegitimate child?). Yet, not once in the recorded pages of Scripture, do we see Abraham and Sarah acting as victims—blaming the world or God for their ongoing hardships and challenges. Abraham and Sarah whined, and doubted and laughed at the promise of God, but never did they lay down and quit. Did they want to? Is the sky blue? Does a one-legged duck swim in a circle? Yes, it is fair to suggest that they, like us, wanted to give up.

Quitting is as much of a decision as to go one more mile on the journey. I find courage in the "Overcome" part of Abraham and Sarah's story. We believe what Christ has already accomplished for us on the cross. By faith, Abraham and Sarah kept moving ahead in their journey as the story unfolded—one day at a time. Wherever life has brought you today, let me encourage you, don't quit. Don't give up. If you can't quite take hold of the Holy Spirit's power within you, take hold of God's goodness and ability to provide.

My wife, who suffers from chronic depression, plays Mandisa's song, "Overcomer" as a ring tone on her phone. I don't think she's alone in relating to this song, as it was the top Christian hit of 2013. The lyrics, written by David Garcia, Ben Glover, and Christopher Stevens, are life changing:

Whatever it is you may be going through
I know He's not gonna let it get the best of you
…You're an overcomer
Stay in the fight 'til the final round
You're not going under
'Cause God is holding you right now
With Christ, you are an overcomer.

U is for Understanding

Life is a teacher. Sometimes it speaks quietly and at other times it comes down on us like a frustrated nun at a Catholic High School. From time to time we all use catch phrases like, "You don't know what you don't know," or "I've attended The School of Hard Knocks" or "I've got a degree from The University of Life", to name a few clichés. But is life always a teacher? Yes. Do we always learn from it? No. Is God always a teacher? Yes. He utilizes the energy from the challenges that come with the journey of life, to grow us as people. Much more effectively than "Life University", where we're pretty much left to our own devices.

Whether or not we learn from God is completely dependent upon us. I would argue that we all know people—you may be thinking of them right now—who haven't really grown as people, or haven't matured in their understanding of life in years. Why? They weren't ready or open to learning. Period.

The story of Abraham and Sarah is a story about a married couple who grew in their understanding of faith and life. Certainly this doesn't mean that they had it all figured out, or that they didn't have any doubts. You know they did. On several occasions, as the promise of God seemed to fade as a possibility, Abraham experienced God's presence in a powerful way. I believe these milestone experiences kept Abraham and Sarah believing in the promise of a future nation, even in the face of the impossibility of having a child. Abraham even lied on several occasions because of his fear and doubts—one of the many evidences for the trustworthiness of Scripture, as it shows even the dark side of this great Patriarch. Scripture records that Sarah laughed at the angels when they said she'd be pregnant in a year. Who can blame her, she was 90! (Genesis 17:17; 18:12). Can you relate? Doubts. Fears. Nervous laughter. Anxiety about the future?

An amazing example of Abraham's spiritual growth involves his only son, Isaac. God's promise came true and Sarah gave birth to a son whom they named Isaac. He was their pride and joy and a constant reminder of God's blessing. Abraham was pushing 100 years old when the next unthinkable thing happens—God asks Abraham to sacrifice Isaac—to kill his only son. What does Abraham do? He obeys. Check this out:

> By faith Abraham, when God tested him, offered Isaac as a sacrifice. He who had embraced the promises was about to sacrifice his one and only son, even though God had said to him, "It is through Isaac that your offspring will be reckoned." Abraham reasoned that God could even raise the dead, and so in a manner of speaking he did receive Isaac back from death (Heb. 11:17-19).

Look closer at the phrase, "Abraham reasoned…" What does that mean? It means he thought through the call. The Old Testament story tells us that Abraham traveled three days to the mountain where he was instructed by God to sacrifice Isaac. Those were three very long days; three days to wrestle with God's command. Abraham *came to an understanding* that if God wanted him to slay Isaac, then he would do it, trusting that God would raise Isaac from the dead. Wow. He reasoned. He thought it through. I'm sure, as a father myself, that he didn't sleep a wink during that three-day journey. He probably laid awake asking a million questions, and coming to one conclusion: the God who gave them the miracle that was Isaac, was also capable of performing another miracle if needed. What crazy faith revealed in a crazy life story!

Let me make this perfectly clear: *a faith journey requires reason.* Life in and of itself pushes us to think about the deep stuff, to wrestle with the interrogatives of life; the who, what, when, where, why, and how. We're all to examine God's promise to "test us" (Gen. 22:1; Jas. 1:3, 12) and personalize interruptions designed by God to see what we truly believe. Does God promise to give us understanding? Yes and no. Understanding doesn't mean that God will explain the "why" of an interruption. More than likely, understanding, like that in Abraham's case, draws us to a deeper knowledge (theology) of God's nature, His unlimited intelligence (omniscience), or constant presence (omnipresence), or mighty power (omnipotence), and how it applies in our situation.

I found myself, in my current, crazy, disrupted life, reminded that God is *good.* This kept me from slipping into despair, which is often the result of believing that God is not entirely trustworthy. If that is so, there's really no hope. Thankfully, God is always good.

Killing Isaac made absolutely no sense, but a lifetime of walking with God helped Abraham reason that God would always do the right thing…eventually. Understanding the experiences of life often comes with time. Most of us don't earn a college degree in months. Instead, it takes years of disciplined and structured study to earn a degree in a chosen field. So it is with life; hopefully we pick up life lessons as we journey along.

Most of us can move forward by looking in the rear-view mirror—the history of our relationship with Christ. By looking back at the times when God worked things out for our good, we're able to face forward and lean into the hot, dry, stinging sands of disruption. We can trust that God not only knows where we are, but He knows what we need and is able to provide. Remembering God's care in the past bolsters our faith for the crazy life ahead. So, put that gray matter to work—think long and deep about your life and about God. As Dallas Willard would say, "get a thought about your thoughts; get a thought beyond your thoughts."[13] Your faith depends on it.

R is for Relationship

No one really ever takes a long journey alone. Living out in the Wild West as I do, the self-made man is still considered a highly respected image and badge of honor. Yet in all my years, I have never truly met a self-made man. Every successful man or woman I know had a lot of help along the way. To suggest otherwise is really a form of arrogance. Humans were created to be together. A friend of mine knows this experientially. She recently took four months off from her busy insurance practice to walk the *Camino de Santiago*, an ancient Catholic pilgrimage route through Spain. She wanted to walk it solo, but found it impossible to do, as she kept meeting and making new friends along the way. Her experience changed her life as she immersed herself in the spiritual discipline of discovery by walking this ancient pilgrimage in the company of others.

In our journey, one of the key disciplines is to build relationships today because we're going to need them tomorrow. In our current disrupted state, my wife and I have had a significant handful of people who have carried us along when our legs grew weak. One couple offered their luxury home for the winter. Other longtime friends helped pay for counseling. One dear sister just regularly showed up with food, movies, and hugs. We got calls from friends all across the nation, and a few supportive e-mails from international friends. It was humbling and lifesaving all at the same time. We, who had given of ourselves to hundreds of others for decades, were now on the receiving end of these acts of grace. I know that they were our safety net. If not for our community of loved ones, I don't believe that we could land back in vocational ministry. We would have said it was too painful and lonely and that we would be better off doing something—anything—else. Life is all about relationships. Therefore, the journey we're on requires friends to walk beside us. A community of friends is like a savings account—we keep investing little by little, until one day we have a large enough to take a big hit and still emerge with our hearts intact.

N is for Nerve

Moving forward by faith takes nerve. A lot of nerve. *Merriam-Webster* says that the verb form of nerve is the "courage that allows you to do something that is dangerous, difficult, or frightening."[14] No wonder we often describe tough times as "nerve-racking."

Several years ago my son, Craig, was home on leave from the Marine Corps. He and my daughter decided to drive over to Montana to go skydiving. I was getting ready for work on the day they were heading out; my wife informed me that she was joining them in the adventure. She asked if I would like to come along. I agreed, cleared my calendar, and joined the family for a fun day of insanity. In case you were wondering, skydiving was never on my bucket list. I don't like heights. I get motion sick. These are two good reasons not to pay money to jump from a perfectly good plane, knowing the quantifiable risk of getting the parachute that won't open and the possibility of the story ending with one's body becoming mashed potatoes upon landing. I was determined to be a spectator in supporting my family in this crazy endeavor.

Off we went. It was a beautiful, clear, summer day as we drove to the jump area just east of Kalispell, Montana. That was when the family all clamored out of our car and began to badger me into jumping with them. I held out until they hit me hard with, "Come on, Dad, you don't want to be the *only one* not to jump…besides, mom's going to do it!" That settled it. I would lose face with three out of four Nelsons jumping and be labeled the "chicken of the family." So like the others, I signed a stack of paperwork promising that I would refrain from suing the company or any of their prodigies down to the 20th generation if I were to die. This only increased my anxiety. Adding to the drama was the fact, (discovered just before takeoff) that a week prior, a major incident occurred where the company's larger plane crashed killing all aboard. No kidding! That's what I was told by a ground crewman when I asked why they had only one plane taking us up one person at a time. Maybe he told me a fib just to get my goat. Well, it worked. He got both my goat and my heart-rate up! That information came with the feeling that "someone had just stepped on my grave."

Just so I don't turn out to be a hero in this story. We were all jumping tandem, with an experienced jump instructor who tied us directly to himself. There was no solo jumping on the first attempt. If I was going to die, it wouldn't be alone, I reasoned. What comfort.

The moment came when we all stood and watched as my son, Craig, went first and safely landed with a huge grin on his face (remember, he was a Marine at the time). My daughter, Carli, was next, and she too landed with a shout of glee! My most anxious moment came when my wife left the safety of the airplane for a downward fall of over 5,000 feet, hitting 80 mph. Thankfully, Disa landed safely as well. Now it was Tony-the-Chicken-Hearted's turn to jump. I was all suited up, climbed aboard the single engine Cessna 180 (i.e., a very small plane with no side doors) and took off to climb to an altitude of 10,000 feet. I was managing my fear (and inclination to grab hold with a death grip onto anything tangible) pretty well until the instructor snapped and locked me in to his gear, double-checked all the harnesses, and began to scoot me towards the open side door. Soon my feet were dangling over the edge of the door 10,000 feet above the blessed earth with my instructor's last second instructions were shouted into my ear—it took all the nerve I had not to say in a really high pitched voice, "Um, can we like, not do this?" With a rocking motion my tandem partner counted off to three and rolled us forward and out the door. Which is a nice way to say we did a controlled fall out of the jump plane. As instructed, we did a slow upside down roll and I was able to watch the airplane fly away while I was falling to earth upside down, gaining incredible speed as gravity grabbed us. Our roll eventually turned me face down and the wind shear was staggering. My face was flapping like a Chinese kite in a windstorm. The trailing chute kept us under 100 mph in order to keep the parachute from ripping apart when it opened due to our combined weight and speed. Previously, the instructor told me that he would tap me on the arm when it was time to pull the ripcord.

I must admit it was a pretty crazy experience watching the lush green earth rush up to meet us. After several seconds, I thought he tapped me—which was really hard to tell at these speeds—so I pulled the ripcord and was relieved that the chute opened. We went from a 100 mph free fall to about 20 mph in seconds, causing every vertebra in my neck and upper back to crack like bubble wrap.For what it's worth, it was a lot of fun. However, I never plan to do that again it as long as I live.

Speaking from experience, skydiving takes a lot of nerve. So does living forward in life. Life will hand us the unexpected, the beautiful, the tragic and the hard stuff on a regular basis. Life's interruptions will make us cower and run or steel up our nerve and jump when jumping doesn't make sense, but you know you've got to do it.

Abraham and Sarah took the leap of faith—much more difficult that than jumping out of an airplane because it lasted their entire life. We know how their story turned out because we have it written in the book of Genesis. But to live the story as they did, meant they didn't know how God's plan for their lives would turn out. All they knew was what it was like to walk by faith day-by-day. Occasionally life serves up adventure, adrenaline-crackling-free-falls. Sometimes, it is long, dull days of walking into the searing hot sand in the desert of disruption.

As Scripture says, the belief of Abraham and Sarah grew to a point where they saw the future. Look what the writer of Hebrews says:

By faith Abraham, when called to go to a place he would later receive as his inheritance, obeyed and went, even though he did not know where he was going. By faith he made his home in the promised land like a stranger in a foreign country; he lived in tents,...For he was looking forward to the city with foundations, whose architect and builder is God (Heb. 11:8-10).

Look especially at these key phrases:

"He did not know where he was going."

This certainly dispels the myth that faith requires God to "tell us where we're supposed to be going..." because it is evident that knowing is not congruent with faith. Let's face it, a lot of life is about "not knowing where we're going." Yes, I believe that God has a plan, but that He rarely gives us the road map. Instead, God tends to show us only our next waypoint on life's journey, not the entire route.

"He lived in tents..."

These four words describe a lifestyle of faith. Why did the Hebrew writer stress this? What did Abraham live in before? I'm guessing that, in contrast, Abraham and Sarah remembered the days when they lived in a house; a house in Ur of Chaldea, one of the largest ancient cities of their time. I'm quite sure that there weren't very many tents in the city proper. After Abraham's father Terah died, God moved them out of a house and into an ancient RV—the tent. If tents say anything, they say "mobile, temporary, simple...." A tent shouts, "flexible."

Could Abraham's honor—being a man of faith—suggest that we too must be flexible and hold all things loosely?

"Looking forward."

Evidently tent living helped Abraham and Sarah realize that everything here is temporary. They acquired an eternal perspective on life. I say acquired, because an eternal viewpoint doesn't come naturally. No doubt, as someone once said, "We believe in life-after-life-after death." Still, many of us live like there's no tomorrow, no future experiences, no "city with foundations, whose architect and builder is God…" (Heb. 11:10).

E is for Eternity

I am writing this chapter from the inside of a luxury home. I gaze at the massive timber frame design and wonder, "If we fallen human beings have the capacity to design and build such homes, what then can God do when it comes to designing a plan for our lives?" Such a thought requires me to shift my focus from "now" to "someday" and realize that any and all interruptions, regardless of their intensity, are temporary. They are just part of the plan.

Somewhere in Abraham's journey he began to see with new eyes— eyes of faith—that looked ahead to eternity. The great patriarch had to develop eyes that looked past his daily challenges in family and business, to a future crafted by God Himself. Scripture says,

> All these people were still living by faith when they died. They did not receive the things promised; they only saw them and welcomed them from a distance, admitting that they were foreigners and strangers on earth. People who say such things show that they are looking for a country of their own. If they had been thinking of the country they had left, they would have had opportunity to return. Instead, they were longing for a better country—a heavenly one. Therefore, God is not

ashamed to be called their God, for he has prepared a city for them (Heb. 11:13-16).

We could all benefit by asking God to help us gain this perspective: to hold the things of this world loosely, especially when things that we value—health, status, career, etc.—are removed. Maybe loss is the pathway to *"longing for a better country…"*?

Y is for Yes

Attitude plays a huge role in our journey through disruption. Let me ask, "While walking out any big disruption, do you have a "can do", "yes", attitude? Or are you one who puts on the brakes and says "No" first?Growing up in the farm belt of Nebraska, I ran across some farmers who demonstrated these two perspectives. Any new idea related to agriculture, was often greeted with a "no" from some, and an exciting "yes" from others. I have observed that there are many people who usually say "no" first, no matter what. So their "no" could actually be a "yes" in disguise, or at least a "maybe." What they're really saying, is, "I just need more time to think about it".

I must confess, "yes" as a first response does not come natural to me. I often tell my wife that I'm a "realist". However, I do admire people who experience life's interruptions with the attitude that says, "This is just a bump in the road," while those with a more negative bent, like me, would see a similar interruption as a steep mountain to climb. Here's the truth: the only thing we can control is our response to life's upheavals, whether good or bad. That's it. We can't control our spouses, bosses, or even God. So we might as well stop trying. All you can truly change is you. Part of changing you is learning to manage your attitude and your perspective on key life events.Long-time, pastor and author Charles R. Swindoll shares about when he realized he was becoming a negative grumpy old man—because his wife told him so! He didn't believe it until he took a self-evaluation and realized that, indeed, he had negative leanings. As a result, Swindoll decided to take a different path and wrote one of his most quoted articles. I include it in whole to encourage you and to reinforce the fact that even the best of us—like the beloved Chuck Swindoll—struggle to stay positive in the midst of life's changes and challenges.

The Value of a Positive Attitude
By Charles R. Swindoll
"Attitudes"

Words can never adequately convey the incredible impact of our attitude toward life. The longer I live the more convinced I become that life is 10 percent what happens to us and 90 percent how we respond to it.

I believe the single most significant decision I can make on a day-to-day basis is my choice of attitude. It is more important than my past, my education, my bankroll, my successes or failures, fame or pain, what other people think of me or say about me, my circumstances, or my position. Attitude keeps me going or cripples my progress. It alone fuels my fire or assaults my hope. When my attitudes are right, there's no barrier too high, no valley too deep, no dream too extreme, no challenge too great for me.

As we come to the close of this chapter, let's be reminded that we talk and write about Abraham and Sarah thousands of years later because their flexibility and journey of faith created a legacy for us. They weren't perfect and neither are we. We are flawed and broken. We are all messed up. Faith in God's goodness and faith in God's plan for our lives, helps us hope and look forward. Knowing that we walk with purpose that extends well beyond our little chronological time on this planet, keeps us moving ahead by faith. Keep pressing on. Keep looking for the city whose architect and builder is God.

Questions for Discussion

1. Describe an "in-between time" in your life where you felt disconnected. What was it? How did it feel? When looking back, what did you learn about yourself and about God?
2. What are you holding on to too tightly in this life?
3. If someone was to observe your life for a year, would they see someone who was focused on the-here-and-now (earth) or the yet to be (heaven)? Explain.
4. What is your basic attitude, negative or positive? If you tend to be more negative, what steps can you take to be a have a more positive outlook on life?
5. If you could attend your own funeral, what would you like people to say about your legacy? If you were to die today, what do you think they'd really say? Be specific and brutally honest. What will you keep doing the same? What will you hope to do differently?

Chapter Five

Elijah's Depression

Experiencing God In The Wilderness

Elijah…went a day's journey into the wilderness. He came to a broom bush, sat down under it and prayed that he might die.
1 Kings 19:3-4

What do Christians do when they hit the wall, run out of gas, or go from a mountain top experience to the desert of despair? How is a man or woman of faith supposed to deal with depression? More specifically, how should a Christian leader handle depression when it comes knocking? These kinds of questions will be answered by this in-depth look at the story of Elijah and how God helped him manage depression. Attention will be given to my own personal story of dealing with my wife's major depression and the journey we've taken to help her get better. Here we will talk about the normalcy of depression and outline some ideas on how to handle its different types.

Depression is a disrupter. It is normal in life. Yet, depression is often treated like a dirty family secret—everyone knows it exists but no one wants to talk about it. I am a leader and I have suffered from depression. I am married to a leader who suffers from serious, chronic depression.

Everyone deals with depression sometime, somewhere in their life, some more than others. I will not be able to unpack all the different levels and challenges of depression, but hopefully I can provide direction in dealing with the "common cold" type. I offer encouragement, and permission, to seek professional help for the more difficult forms of depression from which many suffer today.

I want to begin and share with you my story of my family's journey with depression. A pivotal point was reached on a bright sunny day in March of 1992. We were living in Chandler, Arizona, serving a start-up church. I had arranged for a babysitter to watch our small children; while my wife and I took a short trip to Scottsdale. As I loaded Disa's suitcase into the trunk, a great sense of heaviness weighed down on both of us. This was no pleasure trip. This was going to be a voyage into the unknown. It was a trip of quiet desperation, so to speak. We were about to take a drive to Camelback Hospital in Scottsdale to admit Disa into the Rapha psychiatric unit. She was to be treated for chronic depression.

Our relationship had been teetering on the verge of failure, off and on, for several years. The dynamics that Disa's depression created and my often un-healthy reactions to it were gut-wrenching. We desperately needed help. We loved each other, but untreated depression was stealing the joy from our marriage.

As Disa's depression worsened, and manifested itself through anger and hurtful words, I would often rescue the kids (and myself) and escape by taking them to play at nearby city parks. We passed the time, avoiding Disa. I would hear laughter while at the park and realize it had been a long time since we laughed as a family. Sadness gripped my heart during these times, and I wondered when, or if, things would ever get better.

I found myself alone more and more as Disa's depression manifested itself in hyper activity and wall building. Unlike others whose depression may have kept them in bed for days on end, Disa's drove her to become an overachiever. The woman I fell in love with was no longer living in my home. She was closed off. We were like Newton's Cradle, the physics toy of colliding balls. Every action brought an equal and opposite reaction. If I pressured her to change, then I'd be punished with the silent treatment. Lovemaking had become a pawn in a life-sized chess match. If I made the right moves, I would be rewarded. If I did something wrong, then it was either offered as a duty, or not at all.

I know now that she was struggling with huge doses of self-imposed guilt and shame. She didn't like to have her picture taken because she didn't believe she was pretty enough. She felt like she had to always be "on": to be the perfect pastor's wife, parent, and businesswoman. Her outward reality was in constant conflict with the voice running in her head that kept telling her that she needed to be a better wife, mother, and Christian.

The few times she when shared her struggles with trusted listeners, she heard something like this; "Well, if you had more faith, things would get better," which only lead to more isolation. Our marriage was failing. What had begun as a relationship between two young kids, crazy in love with each other, had come to a point where divorced seemed imminent.

In previous years, when the depression reared its ugly head, Disa was unwilling to get counseling. Her denial that this depression was eroding our love for each other ran so deep that any suggestion that we get help was immediately met with anger and punishing silence. It all came to a head one day when she came into my office (just a few weeks before being admitted) and told me how worthless she was to me and the kids and that I would be better off without her. She had hit another bottom, and I knew what was coming next. She said, "I think I'm just going to leave." I took a big breath and said something that shocked both of us. I said, "OK, if that's how you feel, then let's go home and I'll help you pack."

That statement stopped her in her tracks. She stared at me as if she'd never seen me before. Anger flared up in her eyes. This wasn't what she was expecting. Who was this Tony? He was different. He had never said anything like that before. Truth be told, this Tony was willing to risk marriage, and career, because he reasoned that it couldn't be any worse than his daily reality at home.

Disa stood up in a huff and slammed the office door on her way out. My gut was in knots as I am a classic conflict avoider. When I got home later, the tension was thick and foreboding, like the feeling you get when you're waiting for the other shoe to drop. I found her in a back bedroom and asked what was up. She informed me that she was done going to church and that she was just going to give up…on everything. My suicide training kicked in and I assessed her as a suicide risk. This was a Saturday. I called one of her good friends and asked if she would come over and be with Disa the next morning while I was at the church. I was certain Disa was at risk. I believed that she might harm herself in my absence. Disa's friend agreed to help.

The next day was Sunday, and as usual, I got up and headed to church, but this time with my two kids in tow. They sensed that something was seriously amiss and remained quiet on the ride to the business center where our church held services. My heart was a mess and my head was spinning all morning, wondering what was going on at home.

Disa's friend dropped by the house a few minutes after the kids and I left and told Disa that I had recruited her to stay because I was afraid she was a suicide risk. I don't know all that happened in the next hour or so, but some conversation occurred that crushed their friendship. My family was falling apart right before my eyes. It was horrible and gut-wrenching.

Fortunately, God broke through Disa's denial and a few days later she told me that she was willing to get help. After researching all the different possibilities, from weekly long-term counseling to inpatient intensive therapy, she chose the latter to expedite the process of treating her depression.

All of these recent events were running through my mind as we drove to the hospital. It was a warm day as I loaded our car for the drive north. I was driving our bright red Mary Kay Pontiac Grand Am that Disa had earned in the previous year. At that moment, I would have gladly been driving a "junker" in trade for a healthy wife.

The desert weather was perfect, in the 70's, with blue skies and a light-warming breeze. No doubt some snowbird winter resident was teeing up a Titleist at a local golf course as our red car drove by, completely focused on his retirement activity and unaware of our plight.

We drove North to drop Carli and Craig off at a friend's house. What do you say to a babysitter who's watching your kids because your wife can no longer function? "Hi, thanks, uh, we'll…I'll…be back to get them later, I'm dropping Disa off at the…uh…psych ward…." Awkward doesn't begin to describe that moment.

Disa and I didn't talk much on the 40-minute drive. Traffic was busy as this was tourist season. The atmosphere inside the car was thick, like the air before a Nebraska tornado hits. Every red light was both welcomed and cursed each one, as it delayed our arrival into the unknown. Disa remained silent looking out the car window, lost in her own thoughts. I didn't know what to say, so I didn't say much either. What could I say? "I hope you have a great time?" Neither of us had any clue as to what this in-patient treatment program entailed.

Through a season of struggle and intervention, my wife had finally come to a point in her life where she was sick and tired of being sick and tired. I was no longer willing to live in a marriage dominated by untreated depression. I had never dreamed that this day would come. I had run out of hope, yet deep inside I felt hope rising. I wondered, "Maybe this will help her, and, in turn, help us." I felt like God was tossing us a life-line at exactly the right moment when it seemed that our marriage was going down for the last time. We both grabbed on for dear life.

As I steered through daytime traffic, Disa was seemingly in a trance, staring out the window. It was rolled down just enough for the breeze to tussle her hair. The drive was, at the same time, paradoxically short and intolerably long. As I pulled into the parking lot I could feel the grip of fear crawl its way into my gut. I parked, got out, and opened the trunk, grabbing my wife's single suitcase. She usually traveled with several, but for this stay she packed light. It wasn't a vacation, or a business trip. She brought only what the hospital would allow. I found out later that they went through her suitcase to remove anything she might use to harm herself. It was a humbling experience.

We silently walked to the entrance and began the process of checking Disa into a protracted stay. How long? They couldn't say. Someone came out to escort her back into the psychiatric wing of the hospital. Our personal exchange has been lost to the fog of time and the stress of the day. Did I kiss her goodbye? I don't remember. Did I say, "I love you"? I don't recall. I do remember watching my wife walk despondently away, like a little girl who had done something wrong. I stared for a long time at the door she had passed through, feeling embarrassed, incredibly anxious, and surprisingly hopeful.

Though I don't remember much, I know the drive home was difficult and my head was filled with a thousand questions. Would my marriage survive? If not, would I ever find a job as a divorced pastor in a conservative church? What about our kids? Would they end up with their mother or with me? I shuddered to think about them growing up in a divorced home, because I knew first-hand the heartache associated with a single parent household. What was I going to tell my little mission church on Sunday? Would it go something like: "Hi, I'm Pastor Tony and I just dropped my wife off at a psych ward to be treated for chronic depression… now let's sing, "God will make a way…?" Sunday did come and I did stand before my little church and I did tell them what had just transpired. I did so with a lump in my throat, not knowing how they'd respond. There were about 80 adults gathered that day and in the midst of them God had placed a retired United Methodist minister. His daughter was the church pianist. After I made the announcement, the church went awkwardly quiet, but not for long. He stood up, walked to the stage, put his arm around me and said, "We need to pray for our brother here in his time of need". He prayed. I cried. The church cried, and God cried.

I look back on that moment and remember reeling with emotions; dread and relief, fear and hope. I was keenly aware that God did make a way for Disa to get treatment and that the cost was going to be picked up 100 percent by our health insurance company—no small miracle when I look back at the story. The clinic was faith-based, which made it much easier to convince Disa to accept their treatment. So here we were, husband and wife, pastor and pastor's wife, seeking help. She had checked in and I had driven away.

We really couldn't have been in a better spot. The church was filled with recovering alcoholics and addicts, and I knew that if my marriage failed, that they'd still accept me as their pastor. Better yet, in the intervening days ahead they proved themselves kind and unswerving with their ongoing encouragement. You see, many of them had experienced in-patient treatment for substance abuse and were now set free from decades of misery. Their hope buoyed mine on a daily basis.

How does our story of the disruption of depression turn out? That particular chapter turned out well. Disa was in the hospital for 19 days. While there, she was diagnosed with chronic depression. It was primarily the result of lacking certain chemicals in her brain. She worked hard in treatment, learning all she could about her illness. She was put on medication and, in a fairly brief time, experienced significant improvement. I would like to say that the following years were a fairy tale, but they weren't. We still had dysfunctional relational patterns to address, which we did, with the help of professional counsel. But we were now filled with hope.

The early part of the experience was particularly unsettling. It felt like someone had come into our home and trashed it, tossing everything familiar all over the place, emptying out dressers, closets and secret places. With the help of professional counselors, we began the slow and painstaking process of sorting out garbage from good, rebuilding our marriage and home.

Fast-forward a couple of decades. This year we will celebrate thirty-seven years of marriage. I often share publicly that the first twelve were difficult, to say the least, and the last twenty-plus have been good bearing on great, so we've had more good years than bad. I believe it is safe to say that my wife's inpatient treatment and our follow-up work saved our marriage. Has the depression been conquered? No. It is being managed. Disa still struggles with chronic depression; no…*WE still struggle with depression*. Depression is *our* problem because we are in this together as husband and wife, for better and for worse.

Fortunately, Disa has assumed 100 percent responsibility for her own recovery from depression. She fights this crippling mental illness through ongoing counsel, spiritual disciplines, medication, diet and exercise. To her credit, she has worked hard not to live as a victim, but as an overcomer. She tells her story often through her business connections and we tell our story to our local church and to other leaders whenever we're given the opportunity.

I share this story with you to give hope. If you, or a loved one, struggle with debilitating depression, help is readily available. I also wrote this chapter to tell you the truth; this isn't a chapter offering a quick easy fix for depression, in whatever forms it arrives. Our experience says that sometimes depression comes to stay like a stray cat—ever present and ever elusive and almost impossible to scare away!

Depression is a disrupter. It almost destroyed our marriage and at best could have crippled my future in ministry. Yet, as I've stated over and over in this book, God can take any disruption and use it for His glory and our ultimate good. At the time, we had no idea that our testimony of working through the negative impact of depression would bring hope to so many people both in the church and in Disa's business world. Depression is incredibly common, yet is rarely talked about, let alone treated. I'd be remiss not to point out that there are less severe forms of depression that are a normal response to living life in a broken world.

Depression is a disrupter.

This openness has come with a price. Believe it or not, people have left the church when we share our story of struggling with depression. One such case occurred just a few years ago. One Sunday, we hosted a connection gathering for new church attenders at our home where they could meet the pastor and his wife and learn about the church's vision. There were about a dozen people gathered for light refreshments and coffee. It was our practice to have everyone share a little bit about their lives and families. When it came turn for Disa to share, as was her custom, she talked about her role as the pastor's wife, our children, her Yorkie. Then she talked about her journey with depression. She further shared that it was her mission to help people who suffer to find hope and healing as she has. Her testimony lasted but for two or three minutes and was appropriate for a mixed age and gender audience.

After the group left, we debriefed with the team leader. All of us thought the gathering went well. But later that week, the connections director, who organized the event, got a scathing email from a woman who had attended with her teenaged son. She was appalled that a pastor's wife would share such a story with her son present and that she would never come back to our church because of the perceived offense. What's sad is that this woman's negative reaction is not an unusual one, especially when people learn that depression lives in the pastor's home. It's not the first time we've lost potential parishioners because of our testimony, and it won't be the last. I assure you, we will press on and continue to share our story so that perhaps someone can break out of the dungeon of depression. It was obvious that Disa's testimony touched something deep in this sisters life that she wasn't quite ready to deal with at the time. Our hope for her was that some day, she would deal with the deep hurts in her life and find healing. Disa and I learned a long time ago that "hurt people, hurt people".

Lastly, I also want to offer some advice for loved ones of those who suffer from depression. I want to help you avoid some of the less than helpful comments and behaviors that depression sufferers (and their families) deal with from well intentioned but misguided family and friends (see appendix for more resources).

A Theology of Depression

With depression being so prevalent in our modern world, it begs the question: Does depression show up in the Bible? The answer is a resounding, "Yes!" An entire book can be dedicated to tracing the examples and effects of depression found throughout both the Old and New Testament narratives and texts. Why do you think the Psalms are some of the most beloved and treasured Scriptures? Could it be that David, who wrote most of them, suffered often from some form of depression? Absolutely. Psalm 51 tells of a dark time in David's life, wherein he obviously manifested situational depression related to his sin with Bathsheba. While I could unpack David's brush with depression, I want to turn to what I believe is an incredible narrative that traces the impact of depression on a greatest ancient leader—Elijah. His story offers a glimpse into the human condition and God's response to man's struggle with depression.

Elijah is unquestionably one of the powerful leaders in the Bible. His faith and feats were such that his name would later be associated with John the Baptist, the forerunner to Christ. He appeared with Moses the Lawgiver and Christ in the transfiguration (Matt. 17:1-13). He is mentioned more in the New Testament than any other ancient prophet.

Elijah served during the time of pronounced tumult in Israel—a divided kingdom—when God's people suffered at the hand of pagan kings who strayed from the Lord and an errant priesthood. Elijah's role was to bring the nation back to faith.. God used Elijah by performing amazing miracles: stopping the rain, ending a drought, physical healing, feeding by ravens, calling fire from heaven and predicting future events. He was a effective mentor to his protégé, Elisha. Eventually, Eljah was taken to heaven in a fiery whirlwind (2 Kings 2:11). Elijah did what God asked.. He became revered through the centuries by Israel as the most significant prophets of old. Elijah was truly an amazing man of God. Arguably one of the earth's ultimate leaders, Elijah was literally knocked down by an experience with depression (1 Kings 18-19). His bout with depression changed the trajectory of his life and helped him leave a legacy that is still talked about today.

Elijah's Struggle with Depression (1 Kings 18-19)

Energetic. Deeply spiritual. Trend setter. Achiever. Legacy leaver. All these things describe one of the chief figures in Old Testament lore, Elijah. Yet, his life was disrupted by depression. Let's take a look at Elijah's journey into and out of the throws of depression and its role as a disrupter.

It all began with success.

Success is probably the chief goal of almost everyone you meet. We all want to be successful. I wanted to be a successful husband and father. I wanted to be a successful pastor, gaining the respect of my church family, my peers and my God. While we know that everyone desires success, it often has a dark side. The euphoria associated with success is often followed by depression. Why? The answer to that is probably as varied as the individual. But I think there are some general reasons why depression often follows success. The kind of depression I'm talking about in Elijah's case is often labeled situational depression. It is rarely chronic, and usually short lived. It is nonetheless common and can be rather debilitating.

Success is often tiring because it is usually accompanied by a long season of disciplined effort. Take Elijah and his run in with Jezebel. Jezebel was a nasty pagan Queen who was corrupting an entire nation—using her prophets of Baal. Up to that point in time Elijah had experienced the hand of God in controlling weather, raising the dead and the miraculous feeding a widow. It seemed that whatever he put his hands to he achieved the impossible, even the miraculous (with God's help). Pretty good stuff for a resume of success, I think.

It seems that Elijah's successful life experiences up to this point had prepared him for his greatest spiritual battle, taking on over 800 adversaries—the false prophets of Baal. He's mentally, physically, emotionally and spiritually ready to take on an army of spiritual thugs. Perhaps you remember the famed story of Elijah squaring off with the false prophets of Baal and the Asherah pole. I know it so well because it was a favorite story to act out at church camp. It involved fire! I'm surprised I'm still alive after creating so many scenes of God's fire coming from heaven. I digress, back to the story.

Elijah challenges King Ahab and Queen Jezebel's occultic-religious movement in Israel to a contest on a mountain. The rules are simple: each team gets one shot at getting their "god" to respond in front of the nation. The winner takes all and the loser? Well, let's say they best have their life insurance paid up. To make a long story short, Elijah wins in dramatic fashion: God sends fire to prove that Elijah is a true prophet and that He is the true God.

What an incredible experience! If Elijah were alive today he would be placed on the evangelical speakers circuit as the man who conquered the cults in one fell swoop. This story has all the makings of a great movie. It is David and Goliath-esque in that it is one man against a nasty queen and her minions. It all happens on a mountaintop. There's chanting, and taunting, and ego and pride. The prophets of Baal failed miserably in front of the community, it's Elijah's turn. He doesn't settle for just fire on dry wood. Oh, no. He increases the chances of failure by pouring water on the altar... gallons and gallons of it. He wants the people to know that what was about to happen wasn't some cheap magic trick. Then the man of God calls upon the Lord, who responds in graphic fashion with fire from heaven. I would love to have seen this in person: The Holy Fire of God! Elijah brought it. This had to be his greatest feat to date. This moment in time was scorched into his memory like a lightning scar etched into the trunk of a tree.

What happens next? Bands, trumpets, parades...? Not quite. We see Elijah's humanity—his frailty—kick in. He's threatened by a bitter queen, and instead of relying on the God who sends fire, he turns and "runs like a scalded dog." Elijah, a man's-man, turns yellow. How embarrassing. How unflattering. Previously, he move with the grace of a mounted rider. Now, he runs in fear and hides like a coward. If that isn't bad enough, he has a pity party (1 Kings 19). What does God do? God remains fully present and engaged during Elijah's descent into depression. God wasn't pacing back and forth in heaven, wondering what to do with his star performer. God didn't rescue Elijah right away from his exhaustion. He allowed Elijah to experience depression for a season and a reason. What is the reason? Let me answer with a few question; "When are we often most approachable by God? On the mountaintop? Or in the valley?" I think you know the answer. It's usually when we hit rock bottom that we're most open to getting help.

The reason God allowed Elijah to land here is probably only fully understood in the mind of God. God didn't leave Elijah in his time of need. I want you to consider this situation in an entirely different frame than what most of us have been trained to think in Western Christianity We often mistakenly believe that God wanted to teach Elijah some kind of personal lesson. Instead, I hope you'll see the Lord our Shepherd interacting with an exhausted sheep. In my humble opinion, this story wasn't a picture of a Sovereignly designed lesson plan. It is the beautiful picture of a Father reaching out to a son in need. Yes, there were certainly character defects in Elijah's life that needed correcting. His self-reliant egoism observed in his willingness to take on 800 enemies—alone, is one glaring example. We get so hung up on the academic side of Scripture that we sometimes completely miss the point. Sometimes there aren't clear-cut lessons to be learned. Instead, there are clear-cut experiences to embrace that don't stem from an eternal teaching plan. Isn't experiencing the compassion, and the love of our Father enough? Do we always have to justify ourselves with some bullet-pointed, "God must have wanted me to learn these three things" perspective?

Elijah's narrative unfolds like a personal retreat with the Counselor Himself. Elijah has a close encounter with God in an outdoor setting. A

God, who takes a personal interest in his recovery. Let that sink in a little bit. Elijah's path forward out of depression is simple, but not simplistic. God is fully present in the valley of Elijah's exhaustion. Look at God's holy prescription:

1. Ownership: Own your stuff—this was *Elijah's* depression. He had to take ownership of it and seek to do whatever it took to alleviate the debilitating nature of his depression.
2. Margin: Create some space where no one can find you—Elijah ended up out of town in the wilderness.
3. Rest: Twice the Scriptures tell us that Elijah "fell asleep." Pretty good advice.
4. Eat: An angel prepared a meal for him, but Elijah was commanded to eat—to take care of himself.
5. Self-care: God met Elijah at his point of need—physical recovery. How often are we too focused on the different areas of our lives? This story surely reminds us to take care of our bodies, and the rest will often fall in place.
6. Time: God also moved Elijah deeper into the wilderness—his valley—so to speak. Sometimes we need a long season of rest and reassurance from God before we return to the battle. For Elijah, this meant spending 40 days and nights journeying deeper into the wilderness.
7. Reflection: God renews His relationship with Elijah with a question, "What are you doing here, Elijah?" Elijah could do was recite his activity and state a false belief: "I'm the only one left." Really, Elijah? I think Elijah missed the point. God wanted him to reflect, to think about the bigger picture.
8. Seeking: Wind, earth, and fire. Sounds like a rock band. All very noisy. God came after the noise quieted down— as a gentle whisper. This always makes me pause. God

didn't shout at Elijah, God whispered. So that Elijah had to listen—intently.

9. Confession: Elijah confessed his greatest fears—loneliness and a violent death, later solved by God bringing him a protégé (Elisha) and taking Elijah to heaven in a whirlwind (2 Kings 2).

10. Hope: God gave Elijah an assignment that would meet a need in his life. I believe he never saw his need until this encounter with God—the need for a partner—Elisha. It gave Elijah new hope and purpose.

11. Truth: God countered Elijah's perspective about his situation (I'm the only one) with new truth—there were 7,000 faithful.

12. Follow-through: Elijah did what God asked. He recruited Elisha. He took better care of himself (we don't see a repeat of despair). I wonder, if God hadn't intervened in Elijah's depression and if Elijah hadn't taken God's directives, what would history have recorded?

Elijah's personal struggle and recovery from depression stands like a beacon of hope. His story is our story. Depression is a disruption that God can redeem for His glory, our good and as a pathway to bless the world. I am grateful that Disa was willing to have me include our story, our struggle with depression, in this book. We hope that it brings hope to you and your precious ones (see the Appendix for a more detailed description of depression and ways to address it).

Questions For Discussion

1. What one thing stands out to you in the story of Elijah's depression and God's response? Why does that speak to you?

2. Describe a time when you experienced depression. What were the causes? How did you get through it? What steps would you recommend to others?

3. Talk about the different things that people say regarding Christians suffering from some form of mental illness and their potential impact on them.

4. What steps do you think you could take to de-mystify mental illness in believers?

5. How do you feel about taking prescriptive drugs for depression? Has how this chapter influenced your outlook? Please share.

Chapter Six

Mary's Humility

Living A Life That People Sing About

And Mary said:

My soul glorifies the Lord and my spirit rejoices in God my Savior, for he has been mindful of the humble state of his servant. From now on all generations will call me blessed, for the Mighty One has done great things for me—holy is his name.

Luke 1:46-49

What if God asked you to give up your dream in place of His dream? Here we spend time with Mary, the mother of Jesus and her husband, Joseph, unpacking God's disruptive call on their lives. Mary was asked to abandon one dream—hers—and accept another—God's, ultimately for the sake of others. God's call can be incredibly disruptive. Disruption can be a great adventure, if approached with the right attitude. Accepting God's call can lead us into a living a life others want to emulate. Is it time for you to pursue God's dream for your life? To humble yourself and go where He leads and do what He asks?

Once upon a time, in a land far away, a young couple faced a seemingly impossible "ask" from God, it was an "ask" that would change each of their dreams and plans forever. The Divine request was either the mythical stuff of fairy tales, or it would ultimately change the trajectory of the entire world. The charge was to birth and raise the Messiah. The birth of their first son would split history, and disrupt their lives in ways they never dreamed. Most of the world knows about Mary. Over a billion of us, Christians, venerate her at some level. While I don't take the route of my Catholic brothers and sisters, I do believe that the evangelical world has not considered Mary with the respect she deserves and that God intended. The fact is that Mary, a woman, allowed her womb to be borrowed of her own free will. She gave birth to the One who would save me from hell's fury. This means that I owe her my deepest respect and gratitude. Humanity could not have been saved without the participation of woman and one woman in particular. Mary's choice to bear Christ would wipe out the stain of Adam and Eve's choice to bear sin.

We're going to take a deeper look into one of the most famous couples of antiquity, Mary and Joseph. We'll be looking for the tangible and intangible things that God saw in them to the extent that He knew they'd be capable of handling the phenomenal disruption of bearing, birthing and raising the Christ child. As we'll see, being the chosen of God often comes with a very high price tag. But the price was worth it in their case, as we still look them, to Mary especially as people worth emulating. We will focus on God's disruptive call on their life and how they abandoned one dream—theirs—to accept another—God's—for their life, and ultimately for the sake of humanity. Their story we will be challenged to live a life of profound legacy. God is still working to redeem all of humanity, and has invited each of us into the journey.

Living a Life That People Will Sing About

Inspired by the Holy Spirit, Mary sings, *"all generations will call me blessed...."* At first blush this appears to be an arrogant statement. We know better. We know Mary's life. played out on the Judean stage, as recorded in the four gospels. They tell us that she was truly someone special. You could say that this brave maiden stood at the precipice of faith, and jumped. Mary story is a portrayal of obedience and faith. At the time of the angel's visitation, she was just a young girl, while mature in her learning. Her people were waiting in long anticipation for the coming of the Messiah. It would require incredible trust to accept the role required of her knowing there would be consequences far beyond her control. Mary lived knowing that, through the Holy Spirit, her leap of faith, her "yes" that day, and every choice after—was *for all generations*. She would leave a legacy.

Mary and Joseph have been gone for over 2,000 years. At the risk of being blunt, they're dead. Yet all these years later I'm writing about their life, their legacy. What people say about us past the grave is telling. As a pastor, I've officiated a lot of funerals, and one of the first revelations about a person is how he or she approached life. It's always a great honor to speak last words over those who lived "with the end in mind." This past year I had the privilege of burying Kenny and his wife Bert Coulston. Surprisingly, Kenny, who maintained great health long into his 80's, went first before his wife, dying from complications related to leukemia. He died with several generations of family around him in the house he had built with his own hands from paycheck-to-paycheck. Here's a piece that I wrote for our local newspaper about Kenny and Bert while they were still living.

Faith and the Greatest Generation

I'm a people-watcher. Whether at an airport, the rare visit to a shopping mall, or in church, I like to see how people interact. A few weeks ago during our Sunday worship service, I was sitting in the back of the auditorium observing. As my eyes swept over the room, they landed on a familiar couple. I've known these two for close to 20 years. While small in stature, he was standing large. His grey hair was slicked back in its usual style. He was wearing his church clothes—comfortable dress slacks and shirt. What caught my attention wasn't anything unusual, but something quite ordinary—he was holding hands with his wheelchair-bound wife. Kenny standing, Bert sitting. I couldn't take my eyes off of them. In some mysterious way seeing them together that morning became a moment of worship for me. Let me explain.

This couple has been married for over 60 years. That's 60 plus years with the same spouse. Tom Brokaw tagged their demographic as "The Greatest Generation." While I don't think that label fits everyone born before 1930, it certainly fits these two well. Raised in the Great Depression, they seem to have approached life in a much different and healthier way than those of us born later. In this day of cohabitating and throw-away marriages, their six-decade long marriage covenant shines like the Polaris on a clear night. Through war, depression, recession and life, Kenny and Bert chose to remain connected through marriage and through their shared faith.

As a married couple, they attended and served the same church, together. A church, I might add, that is much different than when they dropped their kids off at Sunday school in the 60's with worship services that sang songs from the 19th century. They're still here, in spite of the change of music, methods and style. I hope that I'm as flexible should I be granted a long life.

In this winter season of their lives, times are pretty tough. He's in amazing health for one pushing 90, but she's in assisted living with failing memory. I think how hard it must be to visit her daily, to bring her to church, and then drive home—alone. I was deeply moved by this simple touching of hands while in worship. This loving gesture made me wonder, "How many Sundays have they done exactly this over these last 60 years?" Probably most of them. Could this be a key to a good, long-lasting marriage? Could love that lasts a lifetime be as simple as reaching out in faith and holding the hand of your beloved? For me this image has become the picture of two souls whispering, "I'm here and I love you." And this, my friends, is a deeply spiritual act of worship.

It was with great admiration that I officiated and buried Kenny Coulston, my longtime friend and elder of the church I served. I wept while reading the story printed above during his service. The list of his good deeds would fill pages and pages. He died just a few hundred feet from the house he was born in, a true native of his beloved Sandpoint. He was probably one of the best men this town had ever produced. He fought in WWII, celebrated almost 60 years of marriage and did what Jesus asked, helping widows and others in need for decades.

But what set this man apart for me was his ongoing *humility*. Kenny loved God, the church, his family and friends, and he was always self-aware, questioning his motives, his drive and often felt like he hadn't done enough. Before you begin to wonder, "Didn't he know he was saved by grace?"—to which I would answer, yes—Kenny also wanted to live his life only to please God. With that, he knew there was always room for improvement. He listened carefully to the daily call of God. Kenny Coulston lived a life of legacy, a life worth singing about.

In contrast, a few others I've buried left families and neighbors who had little or nothing good to say about the deceased. I've sat with family members who were at a total loss for words during the funeral planning process when asked to share something good or favorable about their departed. Imagine living a long life and at the end, having no one with a kind word to say. How does that happen? Both lives involve choices. Who we choose to serve, self or others (and God) makes a world of difference.

Mary and Joseph, early on, seemed to have figured it out. Each day they said yes to God's call and did whatever He asked of them. This was a life of purpose and meaning. It was one filled with political upheaval, danger and disruption but it was a life of wonder and joy. Later, the world would call them blessed!

Being a Person Who is Written into God's Story

Most of us want to live a legacy by being mindful of our days and our loved ones. What does it take to be the kind of person to whom God would assign a mission? Isn't that the adventure we long for? The story of Mary and Joseph is, in some sense, a big reveal. God asked them to step-parent the Messiah. It was a task that would take the next 30-plus years of their lives, Mary's in particular. We don't really know what happened to Joseph. Because he doesn't show up in the later part of the Jesus story, some scholars think Joseph met an untimely early death. We don't know for sure, but his absence in the later narrative leaves room to suggest that Mary raised her children as a single parent.

Helen Keller, deaf and blind from an early age, is quoted as saying, "Character cannot be developed in ease and quiet. Only through experience and trial and suffering can the soul be strengthened, ambition inspired, and success achieved."[15] If Helen Keller's profound insight proves true, then Mary and Joseph ended up developing amazing character. I would argue, however, that they didn't start out in this faith journey character-less. God chose two people who had already laid a foundation of solid integrity and strength upon which He could build. They had already shown God that they were willing and able to take the risk. How so?

Luke's account of Mary emphasizes her chastity. She was a virgin. A a sign then, as it is now, of character and virtue. Three times in the first chapter, Luke the physician, points out that Mary was a virgin. This purposeful emphasis means what it is supposed to mean: that Mary had never slept with her fiancé, her betrothed future husband, Joseph.

Mary's response to the angel from that first moment shows us her intelligence and heart. When told of the miracle about to happen (a virgin becoming pregnant) she was troubled. And she asked a super question: "How will this be? ...since I am a virgin?" (Luke 1:33). The young woman knew enough about human biology to know that it takes two people to make a baby. After learning that the baby would be the result of a supernatural miracle, she did what so few of her people had done for millennia, she believed and obeyed. Her words ought to cause pause for each of us. She simply responded, "I am the Lord's servant, ... may your word to me be fulfilled."

I've wondered what Luke, the writer of this gospel felt. He indeed interviewed Mary the mother of Jesus to get the story straight. Was he awed? Humbled? Curious? What else did they talk about? Oh, to have sat in on those sessions. Luke authored what has become known as one of the finest historical biographies of antiquity for its accuracy and reliability. Imagine sitting down with the mother of the Savior of the world and asking, "Please, tell me the whole story, from beginning to end."No doubt seeing an angel was extraordinary, not to mention an intimate visitation of the Holy Spirit, which ultimately leads to her miraculous pregnancy. Literally and figuratively astounding. For a young, unmarried woman, the request to bear a child must have caused her anxiety, to say the least. She inherently knew that, barring another angelic dialog, her fiancé, Joseph, would surely not understand how she got pregnant. This would put her entire future at risk, quite literally, through death by stoning. I'd call this a disruption of magnanimous proportions. The angel did appear again and explained the situation to Joseph. Still there were the prying eyes of a whole village, so Mary hastily skipped town for a visit to her Aunt Elizabeth. She, also, was miraculously pregnant. Her son would also become famous for he was none other than John the Baptist (Luke 1:39). Mary stayed down in the hill country of Judah for three months. At the end of the first trimester, Mary would no longer be able to hide the pregnancy. So she headed back home to tell her husband the news.

Are you wondering, "Why doesn't God call me into some great adventure?" Maybe the answer is, "You're not ready". Maybe you've got a lot more living to do so you can acquire the character and abilities that God an employ in His grand enterprise of redeeming humanity. Scripture talks about God's disciplining us for our own good, to mature and grow us (Heb. 12:4-13). God is actively searching for those whose hearts are devoted to Him (2 Chron. 16:9). When God finds you and invites you to join Him where He's working, you want to be ready to say yes. Let's walk together through this narrative with fresh eyes so that we can discover God's dream for our own lives and ways to bring it to fruition.

Treasure the Experiences as They Unfold

Luke is the only gospel writer to give us a glimpse into how Mary handled all the crazy life experiences surrounding the birth of Jesus.

After the visit of the shepherds, Luke simply stated, "But Mary treasured up all these things and pondered them in her heart." That little three-letter word, "but" is a contrasting conjunction. Luke was contrasting the shepherds' exuberance, they who had "...spread the word concerning what had been told them about this child..." (Luke 2:17) with Mary's quiet demeanor and introspection. Drawing the reader deeper into the gospel story.

She "treasured" and "pondered" in her heart. I have to confess, as a guy, I have no idea what this means. Women have a mysterious and amazing ability to process experiences that most men don't possess. Mary not only lived her role as the Mother of Jesus, *she felt it.* Mary's memories were attached to deep thoughts. She had emotional and spiritual knowledge with an understanding that most women have, and few of us men comprehend. When my wife says, "You shouldn't really trust that person," and I ask why? She responds with, "I don't know, just don't." I've learned to do what Disa intuitively knows.

Even intuitive women must intentionally be present, choose to awaken and engage fully with God's daily call on their life. We can all learn to be more like Mary and treasure life's journey. Treasure means that you choose to value God's work in your life—even the mundane things—like changing diapers, bandaging skinned knees and encouraging others. Like Mary, take time to "ponder," to think deeply, to meditate, about life's little secrets and meanings.

God is mysterious, which means He can't be fully figured out. Scripture says God makes known His secrets. Our Heavenly Father leaves us clues to His nature, like Reese's Pieces for E.T. to follow. To miss them is to miss Him. Be the kind of person God can call for a great adventure. Disruption and adventure are twins. You can't have one without the other, ever. They will lead you to live a life that you will treasure and others will sing about!

Be Willing to Go It Alone

I often get a sense of melancholy at Christmas. I don't always know why. Maybe it's the short days and diminished sunlight where we live. Maybe it's the brazen consumerism of American culture where they start advertising Christmas before Thanksgiving. Maybe it's the brokenness of my own family history. It is hard to pin down, but I do know that that sense of melancholy leads me to reflect deeply on Mary and Joseph, an unmarried couple going it alone.

Scripture indicates that they went to Bethlehem, per Caesar's order, to register. Rome wanted to know how many people there were in this area (Luke 2:1). It is doubtful that they traveled alone, although it's quite possible. The distance from Nazareth to Bethlehem, via a trip through Jerusalem, is about 80 miles. Tradition has Mary riding a donkey. It was a four-day trip on foot, if you were in good health. It may have been longer due to her pregnancy. I envision them traveling rather isolated, even shunned by their friends and family. Why? They were an unmarried, pregnant couple. Taboo in Jewish circles. Good Jewish girls didn't get pregnant before they got married. Telling people, "God did it," probably wasn't a very good idea either. So, here they were, willing to do God's bidding, at a time when they had to do it *alone*.

This is a much-needed message in today's Christian world where we are experiencing one of the great cultural shifts of values and morality in my lifetime. It is a confusing time when Christians are polarizing over all kinds of serious issues. Western civilization is becoming much like the first century world, where morality was based on popular opinion. We can easily forget that the church was built on the blood of martyrs for the first four hundred years. Christians were hunted and persecuted to death by the Jews and later the Romans. Mary and Joseph set the stage for each of us, with their willingness to be whole-heartedly committed to the Lord, regardless of persecution, as evidenced that by their willingness to bear the Christ child.

Expect to Embrace Disruption

God really messed with the dreams of Mary and Joseph, even before they were to be married. Scholars usually agree that first century Jewish girls all dreamed about being the mother of Messiah. It was talked about, discussed and became a wish and a prayer, "Lord, pick me!"

As I was reflecting on the earliest part of their recorded relationship, I can't help but wonder if there is something in this story for today's young married couples to discover. The key word that describes Mary and Joseph's rise to historical prominence is, "disruption." Isn't it amazing, when you look back at the Christmas story, that the big "D" word showed up early on. When Joseph found out Mary was pregnant he was going to divorce her? Joseph's world was rocked by an act of God, and the timing couldn't have been worse for Mary's betrothed.

> This is how the birth of Jesus the Messiah came about: His mother Mary was pledged to be married to Joseph, but before they came together, she was found to be pregnant through the Holy Spirit. Because Joseph her husband was faithful to the law, and yet did not want to expose her to public disgrace, he had in mind to divorce her quietly (Matt. 1:18-19).

We don't know if Jesus' earthly set of parents were "in love" with each other, because love was not the basis of a marriage in first century Palestine. Parents arranged these things. Still, it seems from the way Joseph wanted to handle this crisis pregnancy that he cared deeply for Mary and her reputation. Joseph was trying to figure out a "quiet divorce" for Mary's sake. He might have been able to keep the public's nose out of this challenging family matter, but can you imagine how he must have felt on the inside? What if he loved Mary? Calm would not be the word that most men would use to describe their emotional state when they find their beloved pregnant by another.

For Joseph to take Mary as his wife after the discovery of her pregnancy was nothing short of heroic. He could have had her stoned to death. But instead, "he did what the angel of the Lord had commanded and took Mary home as his wife. He did not consummate their marriage until she gave birth to a son. And he gave him the name Jesus" (Matt. 1:24-25). Don't miss the last part of his obedience. Joseph took cold showers for the next nine months. Jesus' future stepfather knew what it meant to exchange his dream for God's dream.

You may have a working knowledge of the Christmas story, but remember, Mary and Joseph hadn't read the final chapter of their life story yet. Joseph took on the shame of his betrothed for the rest of his short life in Nazareth. Where they eventually settled was a small community where everybody knew everybody—and their business. As a man, I'm humbled by Joseph's experience. Life didn't turn out like he thought it would. The early days of his marriage were rocked by God's call on their life. If this was an earthquake, it would at least register as a 9.0 on the Richter scale!We know Joseph was anchored deep in the Lord. He was a thinking man, for he considered what to do when he found out. I have often tried to imagine the scene of discovering Mary's unexpected pregnancy. Mary's been gone for three months, no doubt hiding her pregnancy, and when she returns they have a discovery. Did she tell Joseph before he saw her expanding tummy? We don't know, but it seems that he made the discovery when she was three months along. Can you just see a demur Mary, saying to her fiancé, "Um, Joe, there's something we need to talk about…""I'm pregnant with the Messiah… It's from God.""Run that by me again. God made you pregnant? Yeah. Right. I need to think about this for a bit." Scripture clearly says *"he… considered this…"* (Matt.1:20). How much sleep do you think he got that night, and the next and the next? Scripture says the one night that he finally went to sleep he was disrupted again, by an angel, who said in a dream, *"But after he had considered this,* an angel of the Lord appeared to him in a dream and said, "Joseph son of David, do not be afraid to take Mary home as your wife, because what is conceived in her is from the Holy Spirit. She will give birth to a son, and you are to give him the name Jesus, because he will save his people from their sins" (Matt. 1:20-21).

Here was Joseph's step of faith, much like Mary's offering her virgin womb as temporary housing for the Christ child. The disruption was all about redemption, "*Jesus...he will save his people from their sins.*"This past fall, I was meditating on the Christmas story during Advent, and it hit me that Joseph and Mary gave up all sense of normalcy for their time and place for God. Maybe their own time-line for having kids was re-arranged (they did have more); quite possibly their dreams for buying a home and building Joseph's carpentry business were at best re-directed. One thing can be said for sure; Mary and Joseph's hope of having a "normal" life were forever dashed on the rocks of reality when Mary said, "yes" to the angel. Moreover, we've sentimentalized Mary and Joseph's interrupted lives. In a true sense our Christmas-time crèche scenes are really nothing but dreamy hubris. While we ogle at the hundreds of varieties of crèche scenes that dot a million homes during Christmas time, we forget that Mary and Joseph were *not* having a spectacularly good time. They were abandoned by family and friends and ended up in a barnyard with only animals. To do what? Have a baby—their first. Christ's parents possibly didn't even have a typical Jewish mid-wife to guide them through the experience.Soon after the birth of Jesus, they were warned to flee the land of their homeland. They became refugees in the foreign land of Egypt, the fulfillment of ancient prophesy (Matt. 2:13-18). It was a major disruption that involved traveling a great distance. Thankfully, they had the gifts from the Magi to finance the trip. After Herod died, then they made another long trip and settled in the non-descript town of Nazareth. Joseph set up shop as a wood worker, and Jesus would live there until he launched his ministry at the age of 30.

Was the sacrifice worth it? If you're a Christ follower, it was more than worth it, they saved your life by being *the ones* who helped save the planet through Christ.

Be Willing to Give Up Control

Control. We like it and long for it when we don't have it. In our fallen nature, control becomes a major issue in marriage and parenting. But this faith journey requires each of us to learn to give up control over a lot of things.

As any parent would, Mary, raising Jesus, struggled with the need to control her son. We don't know a lot about the boyhood of Jesus. Scripture goes silent in regard to his earliest years after his birth and flight to Egypt when he was probably two years old. 10 years pass before we see him again. This time he travels to Jerusalem with his family, as was their annual custom, to attend Passover. This was another sign of their devotion to God for they were poor and this was a major expense.

Having raised kids, I truly love this story because it is so intense. These 12 verses in Luke 2:41-52 give us a glimpse into the challenges of raising the Messiah. Mary and Joseph leave Jesus behind in the big city and get into a big fight over the episode. At least I'm pretty sure they did, because know that I would have been in deep weeds had I left one of my kids behind when we were traveling.

They had traveled at least a day when they discovered that Jesus was not among his siblings. Can you imagine the conversation between Mary and Joseph? "I thought you said he was with you? How could you lose Jesus?!"

They rushed back to Jerusalem and it took them another three days to find Jesus. By this time, surely, they were worried sick. The gospel writer indicates this when he quotes Mary's words to Jesus, "...

His mother said to him, "Son, why have you treated us like this? Your father and I have been anxiously searching for you" (Luke 2:48). Can't you imagine this seen in your minds eye? Mary and Joseph had been frantically, desperately searching the whole city for three long days. They probably hadn't slept or eaten, fearing the worst. Where did they find him? "After three days they found him in the temple courts, sitting among the teachers, listening to them and asking them questions" (Luke 2:46). Jesus impressed those gathered around him; "Everyone who heard him was amazed at his understanding and his answers" (Luke 2:47).

The crowd was amazed. His mother wasn't. She felt mistreated. "How could you do this to us Jesus?!" In other words, she was expressing her frustration with having not been in control of the situation. It seems clear that Jesus didn't ask permission to stay behind and debate the experts in the Law. Jesus obviously didn't bother to get permission. Jesus' response to Mary's hurt feelings seems rather cool to me. Staring into her anguished face, he simply asks, "Why were you searching for me? Didn't you know I had to be in my Father's house?" (Luke 2:49). Luke quickly explains in the next verse that his caregivers were a bit clueless. Jesus was not being disrespectful, rather he was making a point to his folks: I will do what God asks, *even if it disrupts your lives.*

Fast-forward another 20 years or so to when Jesus is deep in his ministry. He's healing, casting out demons, and teaching God's Word in fresh and new ways. As a result, Jesus was gaining quite a following. He was constantly being challenged by the power brokers of his day, the religious leaders.

His popularity makes it hard for him to spend down time with family, friends and disciples. His mom hears about it and decides to do something. She takes his brothers with her to go and bring him home:

Then Jesus' mother and brothers arrived. Standing outside, they sent someone in to call him. A crowd was sitting around him, and they told him, "Your mother and brothers are outside looking for you." "Who are my mother and my brothers?" he asked. Then he looked at those seated in a circle around him and said, "Here are my mother and my brothers! Whoever does God's will is my brother and sister and mother" (Mark 3:31-35).

Mary could not pressure him, even with family, to come home. Jesus refused to be controlled, which must have been an incredibly frustrating moment for Mary. She was a mother, after all. No doubt she realized that Jesus was going to do what God called Him to do. The most painful experience with her son was yet to happen on a hill called Golgotha.

Love Deeply Enough to Suffer Loss

From the age of 12, we see that Jesus' awareness of His mission deepened. Christ's mission was two-fold: First, to disciple—train up—a handful of leaders who would be able to advance the good news through the multiplication of other disciples (Matt. 28:18-21), and secondly, to die for the sins of the world (John 3:16-17).

Most of us know the Easter story—the death, burial and resurrection of Jesus Christ from the dead. It is the most amazing story of Good News the world has ever known. But lest we get too familiar with the story, let's remember that Mary's heart was pierced as a result of Christ's call to die.

When Mary and Joseph presented Jesus in the temple to dedicate him to the Lord, they were met by a man who made a prophecy. His name was Simeon and after blessing them both, Simeon turned his attention to Mary and said, "…And a sword will pierce your own soul too." (Luke 2:35). This prophecy came true on Passover, when a Roman soldier pierced Jesus' side with a spear to make sure Jesus was dead (John 19:34). Mary was there—to see the blood and water pour out of her son, her Savior's, broken body. Can you imagine? Seeing your first-born son, entirely innocent, hanging on a cross and suffering in agony, beaten and bloodied by Roman soldiers? How did she do it? How did she handle the jeers directed at her son from her "pastors," the religious leaders of her day?

Simeon was right. When the soldier's spear pierced Jesus' side, it pierced his mother's soul too. The scene is almost too much to bear, so we want to press on to the resurrection. But first, Mary, the mother of Jesus, (and several other women) stood at the foot of the cross. Weeping. Hurting. Devastated. Wondering where God was in all this mess. Even though Jesus told his followers this would happen, they didn't want to hear it or believe it.

In this picture we see a mother's love tested to the extreme. It was tested by God. Mary's faith was tested further by the abandonment of Jesus' disciples in His hour of need. One of the most challenging things that Christians, and Christian leaders experience is betrayal by others. Every pastor's wife I've ever met has been deeply wounded by someone in the flock, mine included. Betrayal by friends and wounding by other Christians is devastating.

One day, when feeling the deep residual wound after leaving our last ministry, my wife said, "You know this hurts so bad this time. I don't know if I ever want to love people again. It's just too hard." She began to sob. I just held her close and said nothing. What do you say to someone whose soul has been pierced?

I had nothing to say. Reason fails when we try to understand the fallen human condition, where people hurt people, often without just cause. Intellectually, I understand the fact that Jesus was betrayed, too. If I'm a follower of Jesus, I'll experience what he experienced. I hate what the sharp sword of betrayal does when it cuts us and those we love. The hurt is often so deep it takes years to heal. Leaving emotional scars at best, and at worst, leaving a wound that never heals.

In these moments, I return to stories like this one where a mother stood fully present in the face of injustice, in the face of raw evil, and didn't falter. Mary, the mother of Jesus, absorbed the blows and the piercing as if they were meant for her. Is it possible to conjecture that Jesus was able to endure the cross because his mother, and a few close friends, were willing to be with him in his greatest moment of suffering? The Apostle John tells us that Mary was "near the cross" (John 19:25). Jesus even spoke to John while hanging on the tree and asked him to care for his mother, which John did from that day forward.

Mary stood near enough to have blood spattered on her clothing. How did she do this? How did she hold up when she heard her son's labored breathing and cries of agony? How hard was it for Mary when she heard her son ask, "My God, My God why have you forsaken me?" (Matt. 27:45). Did she feel forsaken, too?

In moments like this, we remember the beloved passage of Scripture, "For God so loved the world that he gave his one and only Son, that whoever believes in him shall not perish but have eternal life" (John 3:16). Mary saw this played out on the hill called Golgotha and knew first hand the cost of love.

Remember the Resurrection

Mary's darkest hour was seeing the broken body of Jesus. Lifeless. Bloody. 33 years earlier she had wrapped him in swaddling cloths and placed him in a manger. On this day, she laid his body in a tomb. The death of a first-born is the death of a dream. In all likelihood, she had already buried her beloved Joseph. Now she would bury Jesus. What was God up to? This couldn't have been what He planned from the beginning. Disrupted doesn't even begin to explain the pain. The shock. The despair.

We do not have a definitive Scripture that tells us about Mary seeing Jesus after his resurrection. Matthew 28:1 mentions Mary Magdalene and "the other Mary" going to the tomb at dawn. We don't need a Scripture to tell us that Mary knew as soon as the others that her son was alive! Her grief and agony was interrupted and turned into joy! This must have been an incredible emotional roller coaster for Mary the mother of Jesus.

Remember the resurrection. Mary did. She carried that experience, that memory of a miracle, for the rest of her life. God took a tragedy and turned it into a miracle of life. When you're hurting and feeling alone, remember the resurrection. God's promise to never leave us or forsake us came true. When you're wounded and suffering, remember we have a Father in Heaven who suffered along with His son. When you're questioning God's goodness, remember the resurrection. He paid for and erased our sins so that we could have a personal relationship with God (John 3:16).

Belong to the Church

Living a life worth singing about ultimately requires us to be part of a community. Belonging to a church is a necessity, not an option like joining a club. Mary, for all the things she suffered, did not alienate herself or consider herself better than others in any way. God made it a point to have Luke tell the world in his account that "Mary, the mother of Jesus" was counted among the 120 believers of the Early Church (Acts 1:14). She was listed right after the apostles, a place of prominence. She was the mother of Jesus. She had treasured up her experiences with the Savior for over 30 years. There is good probability that Luke utilized her memories to validate the story of Jesus.

Mary was numbered among the Early Church. There were only 120 attenders, so she was known. She was there when the Holy Spirit fell on them, as prophesied and promised by Jesus (Acts 2). Mary witnessed the first wave of new disciples, 3,000 being baptized in water (Acts 2:41). She was part of the assembly who Luke describes this way:

They devoted themselves to the apostles' teaching and to fellowship, to the breaking of bread and to prayer. Everyone was filled with awe at the many wonders and signs performed by the apostles. All the believers were together and had everything in common. They sold property and possessions to give to anyone who had need. Every day they continued to meet together in the temple courts. They broke bread in their homes and ate together with glad and sincere hearts, praising God and enjoying the favor of all the people. And the Lord added to their number daily those who were being saved (Acts 2:41-47).

This is a picture of the primitive church that, in one generation planted churches in almost every major city of the known world. Mary had front row seats. She was squarely in the action.

I know that some of you reading this have given up on "established religion." I get it. I really, really get it. You think you've been hurt in church? Ask any pastor to show you their scars and you'll know that we understand. Churches are made up of broken, messed up people, just like you and me. Don't give up on the church because of human failings. Find another congregation. There is a place for you. Mary, who suffered right along with Jesus on the cross, took communion every Sunday with the other disciples (Acts 2:42). The church is not perfect, but it is the bride of Christ, and He loves it (Eph. 5:25-32).

We need each other. We won't make it without a faith community. To live a life that people will sing about, to leave a legacy, we need others in the body of Christ. We need mature Christians to guide us through disruption. We need new Christians to remind us of where we came from. We need each other so no falls away.

The New Testament books are all written to "we" and "us." Not "I" or "my." It is God's plan for you to belong to a faith community. There is a church that needs your gifts and abilities to advance the gospel. When the church functions at her best, there is nothing in the world that can match her. Even when she functions at less than her best, there is still nothing culture offers that matches her ability to change the world one life at a time.

Believe it or not, my wife and I still love the church. We've experienced our Christian brothers and sisters, the church, coming around us when we felt so discouraged and lonely.. They sent money. They called. They offered their home. They encouraged, confronted, counseled and believed in us when we hardly believed in ourselves. We are on the road to recovery and healing. Yes, we have fresh wounds. They will heal with God's help. Jesus had scars, and his mother did, too. That fact alone gives us great comfort and hope.

Be like Mary. Live a life that people will sing about in the face of disruption.

Questions for Discussion

1. What does it mean to live with the end in mind? What does that look like for you? Mary had to give up controlling Jesus' life and ministry. Where do you struggle to give up control? Share.

2. Describe a time when your heart was crushed by others. How does the story of Mary's heart being pierced affect your view of injustice and wounding? How is God helping you heal?

3. The resurrection reminds us of God's greatest miracle. Where do you need a miracle today? Explain.

4. Mary was an early disciple who belonged to the first church. What does that say about her? What does that say about the need to connect? Share your story of being part of a church (or not). Explain.

Chapter Seven

Paul's Handicap

Understanding The "No's" Of God

"Three times I pleaded with the Lord to take it away from me."
–Paul

"My grace is sufficient for you, for my power is made perfect in weakness."
– God (2 Corinthians 12:8-9)

Why didn't God answer my prayer for healing? Where was God when I needed Him most? When we suffer from a chronic illness or are faced with massive upheaval, we want God do something. What do we do when it seems like His answer is, "No?" Let's take a look at the life of the Apostle Paul from a different angle, particularly his reflections in 2 Corinthians 12. He talks about his suffering and asks God for relief. Here, we find the well-known statement that God denies Paul's request and simply says that His "grace is sufficient". With a fresh spin and engaging story, this chapter explores grace in depth. May those who suffer chronically or live with disabilities of any kind find hope and meaning on this side of heaven.

As a pastor, on any given Sunday, I could look out over my congregation and see suffering and many unanswered prayers. She's got terminal cancer. He's recovering from a TIA mini stroke. He's in a wheelchair from an accident. She's severely undersized due to alcohol fetal syndrome, and so forth. They all have one thing in common. They've asked God repeatedly to heal them and the answer seems to be "No," or "Not now." Over the years I've watched hundreds of people experience incredible hardship. It threatens to shatter their faith at worst. At best, it can weaken to the point of leaving people hopeless.

Let's be totally honest here. We don't like it when God says, "No."

God even said "No" to the great Apostle Paul. I have fallen in love with 2 Corinthians Chapter 12. There, we catch a glimpse of Paul that is rarely seen. We see this missionary struggle with God's answer to his suffering. In this text we can readily identify with a man who was in chronic pain, who turned to the Lord for a solution, and was told by God, "My grace is sufficient for you…" (2 Cor. 12:8). Suffering continued to be a disruptive presence in Paul's journey, probably for the remainder of his life.

Depending on your church culture, unanswered prayer can make life tough for a believer without a Theology of Disruption. What do I mean? The premise of this book is that God can redeem disruption for our ultimate good, and for His glory. Yet, so many of us believe otherwise, including myself at times. We think that suffering is a sign of God's absence, or of our sin and failure. Underneath that thinking is the idea that, as a follower of Jesus, my life should be spared of pain and suffering. *Even knowing that Jesus suffered and died,* we still hang on to the erroneous belief that life shouldn't be so hard—that prosperity and ease equal God's blessing. God's presence. Difficulties must, conversely, mean God has withheld blessings and He has withdrawn. Maybe our lives are somehow even cursed. This ultimately sets many of us up for a crisis of faith.

Please hear my heart. Suffering is hard. It can be debilitating. Affliction or distress doesn't usually fit the formulaic answers that we've grown accustomed to believing about God in American Christianity (i.e., God must want you to learn patience, that's why you've not been healed). Suffering in its various forms often makes us wonder; "Why didn't God answer my prayers? Where was God when I needed Him most? Does He really care?" After all, when we suffer from a seemingly endless, chronic illness or are faced with life threatening situations, we want God do something, anything! The Bible is full of stories of God's intervention in impossible situations. We often make a promise to God that if He would answer our pleas for help with a miracle, we'd give Him all the credit. Yet, heaven remains thickly quiet.

Like a disclaimer before a movie, what you're about to read is intended "for a mature audience." Simply, if you're looking for some cute clichés or a three-step formula to provide false hope, then know, up front, that what you're about to read may be disappointing. If you're ready to hear what God has to say from the mouth of one of Christianity's greatest thinkers, Paul, and his reflections on his own suffering, then I think you'll find some meaningful insight into your current situation. In that, may you gain strength to press on.

I want to begin at the end by asking; "How did Paul's heart get to a point where he was able to look at his acute suffering and say:

Therefore, I will boast all the more gladly about my weaknesses, so that Christ's power may rest on me. That is why, for Christ's sake, I delight in weaknesses, in insults, in hardships, in persecutions, in difficulties. For when I am weak, then I am strong" (2 Cor. 12:9-10).

This perspective is amazing and rare. Here is a man, with chronic suffering, saying that he chooses to brag about his condition because it points people to Jesus working in his life. Really? Is this just wishful thinking? No. I believe that Paul, inspired by the Holy Spirit, was writing about how he learned to cope with pain. Are you interested? I hope so, for it offers a life-changing perspective.

Earlier in this passage, we see Paul's logic. He specifically states that God "gave" him a "thorn in the flesh"... "a messenger of Satan, to torment me...." He reasoned that God did this "...in order to keep me from becoming conceited ..." (2 Cor. 12:7). There you have it, Paul's philosophy, or better yet, *Paul's theology of divine disruption*. Most of us know that God hates pride (Proverbs 8:13). Pride is the original sin of the universe, modeled by Satan in heaven when he fought God for control, convincing other angelic beings to join in this war (Rev. 12:7-12). He lost in the battle for heavenly power and was cast down to earth. He then succeeded in getting Adam and Eve to fall for the same sin. Pride, in all of its forms, is debilitating and cripples our spiritual growth. This is why God acts on our behalf when He sees pride in our lives.

When God saw pride rising up in Paul, the apostle claims that he was given a physical malady to keep him humble. I am not suggesting that this is true in every case, but it was for Paul. It's been true for many of my parishioners. I've actually had people tell me that the best thing that ever happened to them was getting terminal cancer, or having a massive heart-attack, because it brought them back to the Lord. It is with good reason we believe God sometimes allows suffering in our lives for our good. I believe that only God truly knows what we need and can provide a specific remedy to address it. Like a specific drug that only attacks a certain kind of cancer, God provides us a spiritual pharmaceutical to attack the cancers of pride and conceit before they destroy us.Let's get back to Paul. How was he able to reach the conclusion that he did? How was Paul able to say what he said? To answer this, like so many other questions associated with human suffering and pain, we can do some reverse engineering. Most of us have done reverse engineering at some level. As a kid, maybe you tore down an old transistor radio, or a computer, or a car part, taking apart each of its components. Your reverse engineering could have been ripping the seams out of a favorite coat to see how the manufacturer put it together. It's always good to take note how to put it all back together again, with no extra parts left over! The cool thing is that once you've reverse engineered something, then you have a better idea of what the designer was thinking when designing it—at least in theory!

Reverse Engineering

I want to reverse engineer Paul's thinking about the disruptive nature of hardship and its relationship to spiritual growth. My hope is that by doing this, we might be able to look at our own lives with better insight. Maybe we can get a handle on some possible reasons why God has allowed certain things to happen in our lives. But first, it is important to clarify that God is not the source of evil (Jas. 1:13-14). He can redeem evil, as evidenced by the cross of Christ, but He is not evil's author by any stretch of the imagination. God is good.

Here's the big picture. 2 Corinthians is a letter written to one particular church located in the ancient city of Corinth, as well as to the surrounding region. Paul, having planted this church, loved her like a father loves his children. He was grieved that false teachers had infiltrated the church, so Paul was highly motivated to help the church learn the truth about Jesus and the about himself. Paul's authority and integrity were being called into question. He believed that his best recourse was to discredit the false teachers with story of his own. Inside this story we get a glimpse of his understanding of suffering, his theology of disruption, if you will.

A Vision of Heaven

Let's drill down into Paul's story a little. Like a kid dragging his feet into a dentist office, Paul reluctantly tells his audience, the church, that he feels compelled to tell his story; one that he had held secret for over 14 years. His story will eventually be used as a trump card against his adversaries. Paul begins, "I must go on boasting. Although there is nothing to be gained, I will go on to visions and revelations from the Lord" (2 Cor. 12:1). You'll notice a regal humility that runs like a ribbon throughout the rest of this chapter. That's why Paul shifts to a third person voice when he begins in verse two with, "I know a man…." Of course it is a reference to himself. Here's how Paul tells his story of an incredibly personal and powerful spiritual experience that few others have ever had:

> I know a man in Christ who fourteen years ago was caught up to the third heaven. Whether it was in the body or out of the body I do not know—God knows. And I know that this man—whether in the body or apart from the body I do not know, but God knows—was caught up to paradise and heard inexpressible things, things that no one is permitted to tell. I will boast about a man like that, but I will not boast about myself, except about my weaknesses. Even if I should choose to boast, I would not

be a fool, because I would be speaking the truth. But I refrain, so no one will think more of me than is warranted by what I do or say, or because of these surpassingly great revelations (2 Cor. 12:2-7).

Wow! Can you imagine getting a glimpse of heaven? Paul did, and he was not allowed, or unable, to describe the grandeur! My purpose here is not to create another commentary on this critical passage by guessing about where or when this event happened in Paul's life. Rather, it is my purpose to point out that it took Paul *14 years* to get his mind around why this supernatural experience was immediately followed by "a thorn in the flesh." He comes to this startling conclusion; "Therefore, in order to keep me from becoming conceited, I was given a thorn in my flesh, a messenger of Satan, to torment me" (2 Cor. 12:7).

Sharp Edged Suffering

The timing is important here. After Paul had this amazing spiritual experience, he found it indescribable. That must have been something for one who was such a capable writer. A short time later he come down with a physically debilitating and chronic ailment. The very terms he uses to emphasize the acute and painful nature of his illness; "a thorn in the flesh," quite literally, "a tent stake in the flesh" (Greek- *Skolops- a sharp stake*).[16] On the few occasions I've helped my wife prune her roses, I seem to get poked by a thorn or two. Several times, I actually got a thorn in my flesh! I quickly ask Disa to remove it. Thorns hurt! I cannot stand having a thorn, even a tiny one, in my flesh more than a few minutes. A rose thorn doesn't even compare to the suffering caused by Paul's "thorn in the flesh". He's trying to communicate to us that he was in severe pain. A sharp, relentless, "chronic" hurt, like having a stake driven into your body. This, in a time when there were very little remedies for pain.

What was the medical cause of his pain? We don't know. The fact that Paul lived during a brutal time of human history indicates that his ministry took its toll on his body. In fact, in 2 Corinthians 11:23-29, Paul lists his résumé of hardship:

I have worked much harder, been in prison more frequently, been flogged more severely, and been exposed to death again and again. Five times I received from the Jews the forty lashes minus one. Three times I was beaten with rods, once I was pelted with stones, three times I was shipwrecked, I spent a night and a day in the open sea, I have been constantly on the move. I have been in danger from rivers, in danger from bandits, in danger from my fellow Jews, in danger from Gentiles; in danger in the city, in danger in the country, in danger at sea; and in danger from false believers. I have labored and toiled and have often gone without sleep; I have known hunger and thirst and have often gone without food; I have been cold and naked. Besides everything else, I face daily the pressure of my concern for all the churches. Who is weak, and I do not feel weak? Who is led into sin, and I do not inwardly burn?

Interestingly enough, Paul doesn't subscribe his thorn in the flesh to any of these life experiences. He didn't say, "The ship wreck off of Malta really messed up my back." No doubt, most mornings when he awoke, Paul felt like he'd been run over by a Roman chariot! He'd been beaten and left for dead, whipped, shipwrecked, slapped, punched, and chained. I'm sure he had plenty of bodily scars to show his devotion, still he never makes a connection here between his persecutions and the thorn. Why? I can only surmise that Paul's intent was to emphasize that the thorn in the flesh was a type of suffering entirely unrelated to the wear and tear he'd experienced in his missionary travels.

When God Wounds

Paul specifically says he was *given* a "thorn in the flesh" by God. I believe it is safe to say that this experience created a mental, emotional and physical challenge for this great man of God. Remember, Paul was highly educated, an accomplished scholar achieving what is equivalent to a Ph.D. today. He had a working knowledge of vast portions of the Old Testament (the New Testament was just being written), having memorized large sections of Scripture Scrolls. Books wouldn't be invented for another 1,500 years. He held a high respect for Scripture as a Pharisee trained under Gamaliel (Acts 22:3). He had personally encountered the risen Jesus while traveling to Damascus to persecute the Church (Acts 9). This encounter changed the trajectory of his life. He became a disciple of Christ and was baptized like all other believers in Jesus name (Acts 9:18). Paul lived larger than life, yet this painful experience drove him to his mental, emotional, and spiritual limits.

Suffering will do that, won't it? Chronic pain can drive us to the edge of our ability to cope. We can become a person we'd never dreamed we might be; needy, grumpy, and negative.

It occurs to me, that Paul needed a lot of time to wrestle with the implications of his suffering. As a human being, I'm sure he, too, wanted to know "why?". He eventually landed on an interesting answer. The suffering was both to keep him *from* something (conceit) and to push him *towards* something, toward *someone*: Jesus.

To use Paul's exact words: "Therefore, in order to keep me from becoming conceited, I was given a thorn in my flesh…" (1 Cor. 12:7), and "That is why, for Christ's sake, I delight in weaknesses, in insults, in hardships, in persecutions, in difficulties. For when I am weak, then I am strong." What an amazing, paradoxical truth, that has given hope to countless thousands, throughout the centuries.

Years ago, I heard a story from a pastor friend, about a man who'd ended up as a paraplegic due to a motorcycle accident. Whenever his injuries would put him back in the hospital, he'd wear a button that asked, "Are you the one?" When a nurse or doctor would enquire about the button, he'd simply say, "Jesus put me here in this hospital to reach one person for Him. Are you the one?" While many of us might question this man's reasoning, the belief that his suffering had a greater purpose helped him make sense out of his changed life.

Good Outcomes of Suffering

It is amazing that we are given this little glimpse into Paul's deepest personal thoughts. We can take notes from his life, like a student. Whether we wisely apply Paul's learning to our life, however, is entirely up to us. Paul is stating clearly that there are occasions wherein suffering has a larger purpose. As Paul indicates, suffering can keep us *from* conciet, and push us *toward* Jesus. I think Paul would further add that the suffering, the thorn in the flesh, this messenger of Satan (and thus intended for harm), *was not only redeemed, but actually essential to his spiritual formation.* Paul, in his reasoning, seems to suggest that in this fallen world there are multiple agents for suffering: God, ourselves, and Satan. Like a master goldsmith, God shapes it all for our ultimate good and to reflect His glory.

God's Redeeming of Thorns

Understanding the cause of our suffering isn't as important as comprehending and trusting that God can utilize it for our ultimate good. God can even take "a messenger of Satan" and redeem it for His glory and our development. Satan wanted Paul to falter and fail. And Satan wants to destroy your witness. Satan will utilize everything he's learned over the millennia to take us out like a trained assassin.

Prior to his conversion, Saul was an agent of Satan while persecuting the Church. Now, Paul is an agent of Christ being persecuted by Satan.

I am in no way suggesting that all of our earthly travails originate from Satan. I am suggesting that Satan can, and does, inflict harm. If we're not walking closely with Jesus then we're at risk of succumbing to Satan's schemes. The Devil can even take God's gifts and tempt us to sin, as was the case with Paul. He had this amazing vision, yet was tempted to use it to "build his own brand", to exalt himself. God nipped it in the bud with affliction.

In a real sense, I believe, Paul developed his theology of disruption on the fly. As we live life, we are often required to let go of our childhood-god—the "Santa Claus god"—who gave out nice gifts, in exchange for the true God of the Bible. None of us have it all figured out. No one. God refuses to be placed in a box of our design. So, I would argue, that God uses our life experiences, good and bad, to help us see the truth about ourselves, the truth about Him and the truth about the world. This is the foundation of good theology: the study of God. The longer we live life, even with our eyes open and brains engaged, the less we truly know about our God and ourselves. Why? We realize how much that we simply do not know about God and ourselves. We realize our need to trust God all the more. These discoveries can anchor us during the worst of storms.

The movie "Rudy" is a story about an undersized young man who dreams of playing football for Notre Dame. There is a powerful scene where Rudy has a heart-to-heart talk with a Catholic priest inside of the campus cathedral. Rudy shares with the priest his frustration with life, thinking he hasn't prayed enough, or worked hard enough, wondering if any of it is making any difference. The priest says, "Praying is something we do in our time, and the answers come in God's time."

Forming a Healthy Theology of Suffering

Paul, the missionary was living a hard life, ushering in the Kingdom of God by preaching the gospel of Jesus Christ from city to city. Like many, he was familiar with hard work, blue-collar living. He eked out a livelihood making tents with his hands, probably from the skins of animals. A "not-so-glorious-career" for a former Pharisee. We get glimpses of Paul's evolving theology of disruption from interesting sections of other letters written to the church. In the book of Romans Paul describes the formative nature of suffering within the context of a relationship with God:

> Therefore, since we have been justified through faith, we have peace with God through our Lord Jesus Christ, through whom we have gained access by faith into this grace in which we now stand. And we boast in the hope of the glory of God. Not only so, be we also glory in our sufferings, because we know that suffering produces perseverance; perseverance, character; and character, hope. And hope does not put us to shame, because God's love has been poured out into our hearts through the Holy Spirit, who has been given to us (Rom. 5:1-5).

Paul continues this line of reasoning (and faith) as he points out that the result of God's disruptive behavior in a Christians' life. It can lead them into a relationship that cannot be broken:

> Who shall separate us from the love of Christ? Shall trouble or hardship or persecution or famine or nakedness or danger or sword?… No, in all these things we are more than conquerors through him who loved us. For I am convinced that neither death nor life, neither angels nor demons, neither the present nor the future, nor any powers, neither height nor depth, nor anything else in all creation, will be able to separate us from the love of God that is in Christ Jesus our Lord (Rom. 835-39).

Knowing Christ

As a highly educated Roman citizen, Paul had achieved a lot in his young life before Christ. He could have taught and worked almost anywhere he chose. Yet, he was willing to let it all go for something better. He states,

> But whatever were gains to me I now consider loss for the sake of Christ. What is more, I consider everything a loss because of the surpassing worth of knowing Christ Jesus my Lord, for whose sake I have lost all things. I consider them garbage, that I may gain Christ and be found in him, not having a righteousness of my own that comes from the law, but that which is through faith in Christ—yes, to know the power of his resurrection and participation in his sufferings, becoming like him in his death, and so, somehow, attaining to the resurrection from the dead" (Phil. 3:10-11).

What was *the* most important thing in Paul's life? His letter to the church at Philippi clearly underlines Paul's highest value: "I want to know Christ—yes, to know the power of his resurrection and participation in his sufferings, becoming like him in his death, and so, somehow, attaining to the resurrection from the dead" (Phil. 3:10-11).

Paul wanted to know Jesus, and knew that this path included suffering. Paul got it right. That's how he deepened his walk with Christ. It is how we deepen our walk with Jesus also: along the avenue of hardship and suffering. I have a lot of friends through the years who are recovering addicts. While I would never wish to personally experience a substance abuse problem, I have often longed for their desperate dependence on Jesus. For many of my friends, a relapse could mean death. They cling to Jesus with both hands, for fear that they might return to their old ways. They've suffered much, some admittedly by their own hands and others at the hands of demons. They have leveraged that hurt into deep faith.

Could this be what Paul is trying to tell us? We are to love Jesus, to hold on to Jesus as if He were a life-buoy thrown to us while our ship was going down in a violent sea.

Paul, like you and me, was figuring life out as he went along. This learning wasn't just handed to him by some great vision or revelation. Rather, much of his wisdom came through the agony and hardship of a crazy life, through blood, sweat and tears. Can you relate?

Paul's Crazy Life

I love the humanity of Paul revealed in this second letter to the Corinthians. Consider the book of Acts where Paul's conversion and subsequent missional life is recorded. It reads like an action novel, with Paul as the protagonist. His character going from city to city, often causing riots for Christ, becoming one of the most known men of his day. Paul lived a crazy life. I've always had a hard time relating to Paul, the super-Christian, who goes 110% for Jesus. He was very autonomous by nature. God knew this and helped Paul address this character defect by creating an environment—a wounding—where Paul became increasingly dependent on God for help. The more he hurt, the more he leaned into God.

What did he find there? Grace. How did he find it? Through prayer. Paul himself testifies, "Three times I pleaded with the Lord to take it away from me" (2 Cor. 12:8). Most scholars agree that Paul wasn't counting how many times he prayed, but was emphasizing that he prayed a lot about the suffering. Why? He wanted God to take it away! He "pleaded" with God. He begged, he cried, he wailed. I can better relate to this Apostle than the one who seemed more like a Super-hero.

Today, maybe you are suffering. The only healthy place to take it is

> God will always match the hurt with helping grace.

prayer. Let the pain drive you to your knees. There we connect with the doctor of our souls, who administers grace. We can pray, "Lord, take it away" a thousand, even a million times, and God may say, "OK, I will." But if He doesn't remove the pain, God will always match the hurt with helping grace. Every time.

When God is All You Have

I've lost count of the number of times I've visited people in their homes, or in a hospital, or a nursing home, and saw the pain and despair in their eyes. As a pastor, I knew they wanted me to pray for a miracle. It rarely came. Quite frankly, it was these repeated experiences that almost swept away my faith, like an avalanche on a steep mountain pitch. God's silence, His seeming aloofness, ripped out my poor belief systems and left a gaping hole which He slowly filled in with a biblical theology of disruption. A better way to say it, is that I met Jesus in the midst of my own anguish and He became enough. Suffering *can* cause healthy spiritual formation. It did for Paul. It did for me. It can for you.

It is comforting to know that God did answer Paul's prayer. God spoke to Paul's suffering in a way that transcends the ages. God's word here is utterly amazing and worth meditating on for the rest of our lives. Let's package Paul's request and God's answer together again; "Three times I pleaded with the Lord to take it away from me. But he said to me, 'My grace is sufficient for you, for my power is made perfect in weakness'" (2 Cor. 12:9).

How many times have we heard this quoted in a sermon, or seen on a greeting card or heard it from the mouth of a friend? Read it closely. God says to Paul, and He says to you;

- *My grace...* God's gift... God's love... God's presence. Undeserved gratuity, permission to try again...

- *Is sufficient for you…* there are no limits here. God's grace is sufficient to match your hurt, your grief, your despair, your frustration, your anger, your lack of faith… in the present moment…
- *For my power…* this is the God who made the universe, breathed life into the nostrils of the first man and woman, who raised Jesus from the dead, who is all the "Omni"—all powerful (Omnipotent) working on your behalf…
- *Is made perfect in weakness…* We aren't as capable as we like to think we are. What blessed rest it is to know we can be like little children in the presence of the Almighty. We need Jesus. When He shows up in our weakness, He gets the credit for everything.

As if reading our minds, Paul, the great thinker, makes the application easier for us by further unpacking his belief:

Therefore, I will boast all the more gladly about my weaknesses, so that Christ's power may rest on me. That is why, for Christ's sake, I delight in weaknesses, in insults, in hardships, in persecutions, in difficulties. For when I am weak, then I am strong (2 Cor.12:9-10).

Both Paul and God are saying; *"It's not about you. It's always about God".* We've bought in to the lie that Christian maturity is becoming "independent," but it's quite the opposite. Christian maturity is a growing awareness of our weaknesses and a deepening determination to be wholly dependent on God. Sometimes the only way we can learn this is through the grace of hardship and suffering. With all that Paul knew and could reason, his testimony came down to a simple phrase: God's grace is sufficient for me.

This is the foundational principle and the bedrock of this book: God, and God alone, knows what we need *and only He knows* how to meet that need. God, the Great Psychologist knows the complexity of our emotions, our motives and our drives. God, the Great Physician, knows our health needs and can anticipate where our current dietary habits might lead us. God, our Spiritual Director, sees the whole person, body, mind and spirit. He alone has the ability to address our complicated needs with His divine solution.

God, the Great Anticipator, is constantly working upstream on our behalf. God knows what is best for us *before we do*. We can only see the water passing by that's right in front of us. It is water that has already been touched by God. The Genesis record shows us a God who creates good things and who does not leave, but rather invests Himself in the personal and ongoing development of humanity, for the good of the individual, which ultimately blesses the world.

Questions for Discussion

1. Describe a time in your life where you suffered for an extended period of time. How did it impact your thinking, your emotions and your spiritual life?
2. Have you come to a place in your life where you gave up on your faith? Explain. Where are you at now in your faith journey? Explain.
3. What part of Paul's story do you relate to the most? Explain.
4. What part of Paul's thinking, revealed in this passage of Scripture, helps you the most? The least? Explain.
5. Explain your theology of suffering.
6. Where do you need Jesus in your life today?
7. What has God said to you about your current situation?

Chapter Eight

Jesus' Presence

Redeeming Disruptions

"Who is this? Even the wind and the waves obey him!"
—Jesus' Disciples (Mark 4:41)

"Why is life so hard? I have faith, I give, I go to church and my life is still a series of struggles. I just don't get it." If you've asked these kinds of question, or had similar thoughts, then you'll want to look at the life of Christ, closely. We often think that when life became agonizing for Jesus, He stepped into a proverbial phone booth and donned His divinity suit to overcome the obstacles at hand. Here, we get up close and personal with Christ's humanity.

We will look at how it relates to the disruptions that came to him throughout his life on earth and what that means for us.

We've looked at several major Old and New Testament characters and their respective crazy lives. They journeyed through life's disruptions without losing their faith. Now, we turn to Jesus, with special focus on His humanity. We evangelicals prefer talking about Jesus' divinity, His God-ness, to the point that we often miss the essence and encouragement of the Incarnate One, the flesh and blood Jesus. He showed us how to live. Dr. Dan Brunner says, "If Jesus wasn't fully divine, he could not save us; if he wasn't fully human, we could not follow him."[17] God became flesh and lived among us—among our crazy lives. Why? So that we could never say, "God doesn't get it. He doesn't know what it's like down here in our messed up and broken world." The Word, Who became flesh, gets it. He was one of us. The Gospels show us over and over again a Savior who not only embraced, but fully entered into disruption— in person. He didn't avoid, evade, or minimize His own suffering, or that of others. Instead, Jesus *entered in* to be with us. *Emmanuel is in the disruption.* When your world gets turned upside-down, know that Jesus is hanging in there with you.

> The clarifying question that orbits around our lives like a planet around the sun is this: "Is disruption my friend or enemy?"

Life is often troublesome and interwoven with upsets. What we choose to do with that hard truth will determine whether we allow disruption to form us and to grow us; to shape us for the glory of God, and for our ultimate good, or leave us bitter, old people. The clarifying question that orbits around our lives like a planet around the sun is this: "Is disruption my friend or enemy?"

The question of friend or foe brings us face to face with the amazing person of Jesus. We know Jesus came to save us from eternal separation from God, but how did Jesus interact with political upheaval, racism, sexism, plagues, hate, poverty, power struggles, and refugees? What did Jesus do with disruption? How did he respond to it and utilize it? At the risk of over simplifying the depth of this question in Christ's life, *Jesus befriended disruption.* More importantly, Jesus was present at the Creation of the universe and is in the business of restoring and making all things new. He redeems disruption for God's glory, and for His own good, and for us.

As I sat reflecting on how to approach this broad topic in a narrow chapter, I realized it is akin to trying to capture the beauty of the Grand Canyon in a "selfie." Impossible. Yet, I've decided that the concept of taking a "selfie" isn't such a bad idea. I want to zero in on one shared experience between Jesus and His disciples. Instead of trying to fit the "Grand Canyon" into one picture, this chapter will drill down on one particular day in the life of Christ, a day of significant interruption. This day will show us that Jesus is the Redeemer of Disruptions.

It all happened at the Big Lake, the Sea of Galilee. Three of the four gospel writers record this event, so it was one of the many experiences they had with Jesus that left a lasting impression. I first learned of the timeless story in Sunday School. Most of you reading this will be familiar with the cast and crew. Don't let your familiarity with the story block an exciting new message from the heart of God. In Mark's account, 4:35-41, my Bible translation has the heading: "Jesus Calms the Storm." Remember this one?

That day when evening came, he said to his disciples, "Let us go over to the other side." Leaving the crowd behind, they took him along, just as he was, in the boat. There were also other boats with him. A furious squall came up, and the waves broke over the boat, so that it was nearly swamped. Jesus was in the stern, sleeping on a cushion. The disciples woke him and said to him, "Teacher, don't you care if we drown?"

He got up, rebuked the wind and said to the waves, "Quiet! Be still!" Then the wind died down and it was completely calm. He said to his disciples, "Why are you so afraid? Do you still have no faith?" They were terrified and asked each other, "Who is this? Even the wind and the waves obey him!"

The Story Within the Story

To get a good grip on this true story, it is important to understand that it's a story within a story. Jesus had just finished teaching large crowds on the East side of the Sea of Galilee. The Gospel of Mark records some of Christ's parables, earthly stories with heavenly meanings: The Parable of the Sower, A Lamp on a Stand, The Growing Seed, and the Mustard Seed, to name a few. These are little stories foretelling about something big, the Kingdom of God, a Kingdom of influence. In a real sense, Jesus is putting Satan, the current ruler of the air (Ephesians 6), on notice that things are about to change, forever. The Kingdom of God, seemed so tiny at this point, made up of just Himself, His future apostles, and a handful of true disciples. One day it would explode in unstoppable power and influence.

Interestingly enough, the average person attending these large teaching events seemed dearth. Mark writes, "With many similar parables Jesus spoke the word to them, as much as they could understand. He did not say anything to them without using a parable. But when he was alone with his own disciples, he explained everything" (4:33-34). Jesus was investing in the few, making sure they understood His word and mission. It is a story rife with disruption, of every style and form. This is the same stuff that all good stories are made of: conflict, mounting suspense, intrigue, and obstacles. Let's take a look:

"*That day* when evening came…"[18]

"*That day…*" was no ordinary day; instead it was, *That day*. "That day" divides life, before and after. Remember, this story was so significant it appears in three of four gospel accounts. We refer to life changing experiences the same way. When talking with family or friends about some past experience, good or bad, we'll often start with, "Remember *that day* when…." Then we fill in the story: that day when we were married, gave birth, got a promotion, or dad died." That day! Of all the life experiences we have, there are just a few days when we had an experience that we'll never forget.

You may be right in the middle of a future that day, one that will be seared into your memory like a branding iron's mark. These experiences are always some form of positive or negative disruption; without exception. The gospel writer, in a very simplistic way, is giving us a heads up. Something life changing is about to happen on that day, when they had just wrapped up teaching, and it was getting dark.

Evening was fast approaching and the gospels tell us, in brevity, that Jesus was ready, to relocate. The gatherings had become so large, and Jesus so popular, that He had to teach from a boat, just off shore. He could be more visible and better heard, the sound amplified off the water. Getting into a boat gave Him space from the crushing crowd.

Teaching and preaching is exhausting. I know this from personal experience. Most pastors of larger churches are now teaching multiple times on any given weekend and report that by the close of the final service, they're pretty much ready to crash and rest. Jesus, the Man, no doubt, experienced this kind of complete exhaustion, body, mind and soul. We read in the story that Jesus fell asleep, and remained asleep even during a storm, a sure indicator of the depth of His fatigue.

But, I'm getting ahead of the story. After a successful day teaching, Jesus simply said,

"Let us go over to the other side."

While floating in the blue water of the Sea of Galilee, Jesus tells his disciples to head out to the Eastern side of the lake. Some of us like to read the last chapter in a novel so we know how it turns out. Therefore, I think it's important to know that in the next chapter, Mark 5, Jesus and his disciples get out of the boat only to meet one of the scariest, most messed up people recorded in the New Testament! We never learn his true name, but we discover that he was possessed by a legion of demons; thousands of fallen angels. That is the bookend to this story. Teaching crowds on one side, crossing over, and then meeting a crazy, demon-possessed man. He's also about to experience a day he'll never forget. As storytelling goes, what happens in the middle, the boat ride, is vitally significant.

There is a time to stay. There is a time to leave and head out on a new adventure. When asked, "When do we usually feel most alive?" I have been known to answer, "On the front end of an adventure, of course!" As a friend once told me, "Adventure is just a nice word we put on an experience that almost killed us!" This was certainly a reality for the group of rag-tag followers of Jesus. The request made by Jesus wasn't profound in any way. It was simply a directive that communicated invitation. They had been together on the east side of the lake, and now it was time to go over to the West side. No big deal.

They had sailed this stretch of lake a hundred times. So, they pulled up anchor and unfurled the sail and headed out.

"Leaving the crowd behind…"

Jesus knew it was time to go. He was leaving a crowd of people who loved Him, who loved his teaching, who wanted more. If this had happened to a pastor today, he would have launched a building program to house the growing number of followers. Leaders today often get caught up in trying to capture and contain what God has brought, instead of listening for Jesus' next assignment. I know. I probably stayed too long in my last ministry. I was comfortable, had a steady paycheck, and liked being a big fish in a small pond. Yet, deep inside, I felt stuck. I was often bored. Was it a "God-whisper" informing me that He had a new experience waiting for me just across the lake? I guess I'm about to find out. As I sit here writing this, I have just moved to a new place and accepted new ministry responsibilities.

"They took him along, just as he was, in the boat…"

Christ's disciples did what He asked and set sail. They didn't even row into shore to grab gear. They went as they were. They were traveling light. It is always a good idea to include Jesus in your life plans. More importantly, we need to keep Him close. Remember, this change of venue wasn't the disciples' idea. It was His. They were capable and willing. They knew how to sail. Very importantly, they trusted their teacher and friend. Relationships are like that. Spend enough time together and you will discover a person's trustworthiness.

Adventure also attracts others. Mark indicates that "There were other boats with him…" (Mark 4:36) Why not? Who wouldn't want to follow along? I find it curious that no one was named here. So, who was in the boat? At least seven of the twelve chosen ones were fishermen. No doubt they were handling the boats. They were doing what they knew, sailing on the sea.

Don't you love the fact that Jesus, who was "taken just as he was," takes *us* just as we are? He loves to ride along with ordinary people and those marginalized by life. What happens next shakes His disciples to the core. Mark's account says that,

"A furious squall came up, and the waves broke over the boat, so that it was nearly swamped."

This was no ordinary squall. These hardy fishermen had seen their fair share. This storm was a nasty, one as indicated by the language. The English translates it as a "furious or angry squall." The beloved KJV uses the word "fierce." The Greek text (from which we translate the

English) uses the word, *megas,* from which we get the word, *mega.* It was a *mega squall*—dangerous, unpredictable and downright terrifying. These fishermen and sailors grew up on this great inland sea and heard many a tale about men who had lost their lives in storms like this. It was a killer. This furious storm was going to test their skills and the quality of their boat's build.

I enjoyed watching "Deadliest Catch" on the Discovery Channel. I liken the show's salty sea Captains to Peter and Andrew. Self-reliant. Tough. Hard working and fearless. Yet, on this show, you can see the fear in the captain's eyes when the Bearing Sea gets ugly and tosses 40-50 foot waves with gale-like force. This, in my opinion, is similar to what's happening in this gospel story. Jesus' disciples met their match in the mega-squall.

We know how the story turns out: no one was lost at sea. Put yourself in the crew's sandals. They didn't know how this story was going to end. These brawny men were fully engaged and fighting for their lives, trying to keep the bow pointed at the waves. If they messed up and the vessel slid sideways for just an instant, she'd be swamped and they'd drown. They were taking on water, as it was. The ship was handling miserably, taking on water. Two thousand years ago, no Coast Guard helicopters were standing by ready for rescue, no life preservers to float them to safety. Their bilge pump was probably a clay pot. They were in deep, deep water.

Isn't this just like life? Just when things are going well, you experience a little success, a flash flood in the desert roars in, bearing down out of nowhere. Soon, you are just trying to hang on, while getting tossed and bashed about, with the threat of being drowned. On the heels of a successful teaching campaign, Jesus lead his followers straight into an experience that shocks and drenches them to the core. I'm not being melodramatic here. It's in the story. It's in life. It happens all the time.

Why? Maybe a better question is: "Where do these storms originate?" If I could answer that to everyone's satisfaction, I'd have huge crowds following *me*! Some scholars believe this particular recorded storm was sinister. That its origin wasn't a "what" but a "who", Satan. This is a deduction from observation, because none of the gospel writers who recorded the original story (Matthew, Mark, and Luke) give Satan credit. However, the possibility remains, via a by-line to the headline.

Does it matter? Yes and no. If the gospel writers would have identified the causal agent as Satan, then the story wouldn't have had as broad an impact. Maybe Satan's involvement was omitted to make a point: it doesn't matter who brings the storm because Jesus is Master! Jesus is Redeemer! He has the ability to confront, and calm the sea. This is the miracle.

Why do I bring up Satan's possible involvement here? To remind us that we were born into a world at war. A broken and bloody world. The evening news reminds us daily of this fact. Reporting on murders, robberies and terrorist attacks. If Jesus' return is delayed, we will die in this world, still at war.

Without being sensational or morbid, I want to push you to adopt a healthy theology of disruption. Jesus said, "In this world you will have trouble" (John 16:33). As a pastor, I've provided spiritual guidance for hundreds of people, many of whom were shocked and sought me out because they were faltering. They were not only traumatized, but stunned, totally unprepared for "when the roof fell in." There was an untimely death. Their spouse decided to leave. Their company downsized them out the door right before retirement. I'm squarely in the plot structure, too. However, I'm no longer quite as taken off-guard by troubles.

Previous storms in my own personal and professional life drove me to the brink of atheism. Earlier in my life, I reasoned that if God was God then I, and those I love, wouldn't have to deal with so much crap. Yes, I said "crap". Crap, crappity-crap is the word I'm choosing when there are actually other more colorful words that I could dig up. I'll bet you dimes to donuts that foul language was being tossed about by these salty disciples, caught in the mega-storm of the century. Apt descriptors tend to fly when life's fierceness catches us off guard.

Didn't Jesus see this storm coming? Who knows? Probably not. But wasn't He God? Yes. A limited God—limited by His own choice, by His skin, by His humanness. Now, before you throw rocks, take a breath here. I mentioned at the top of this chapter that I wanted to emphasize Christ's humanity. This is not a theological debate, wherein we split hairs to make ourselves feel better about the box we've put God in. People in our churches sometimes even walk away from their faith because no one told them life was going to be hard and disrupted for a Christ follower. We are studying the story where the disciples of Jesus got caught in an unexpected and violent situation. One they didn't see coming. Jesus invited them to go with Him and all hell breaks loose, literally. I believe Satan was trying to stop this radical, young movement in its infancy, by drowning the Leader and His disciples.

Friends, we too, have an adversary. Satan seeks nothing less than our total annihilation. He wants you to flail in the rip-tide until you drown spiritually. He wants to take you out. Period. Peter, who was probably in the boat with Jesus, later wrote to his flock; "Be alert and of sober mind. Your enemy the devil prowls around like a roaring lion looking for someone to devour" (1 Pet. 5:8).

What unexpected typhoon are you facing today? Financial pressure? Career crisis? Conflict with a beloved? Church leaders, including elders, deacons, or trustees would be wise to focus more on preparing their flock for the squalls of life than arguing about budgets. We are to mature into godly men and women, who can weather these kinds of conditions so that we, in turn, can then offer hope and counsel to those who are drowning. Our only hope is Jesus. Speaking of Jesus, where was He in this unforgettable storm?

"Jesus was in the stern, sleeping on a cushion."

Talk about a crazy scene. The disciples are bailing like mad, trying to save their skin, and their Rabbi is bunked out in the back, fast asleep. Take in the picture. Turn it around in your mind. Feel the sting of water hitting you in the face. Feel the heaviness of your clothes as you're soaked to the bone, and your pulse is reaching epic beats per minutes. Then you discover that your leader is snoozing like a baby in the back of the boat, the boat that you've barely managed to keep afloat. Incredible.

This pivotal scene of the story, Jesus sleeping in the midst of a life threatening storm, pulls back the veil on my personal experience with Christ. I don't mean that in a fanciful, "Pollyanna" sort of way, either. If we live long enough as Christ's disciples, most of us are going to go through something so challenging that we will wonder if God fell asleep on the job. For some, if we're totally honest here, we're still angry at God. For all we can tell, He didn't show up when things got bad.

There is another way to view this sleeping Messiah. He was so at peace with life that, even in the midst of a ferocious storm, He wasn't worried or afraid. He was relaxed when everyone else was tense. He was at rest when everyone else was in panic mode and doing their utmost to solve the problem. He was willing to let those around him do everything in their power to solve their problems until they ran out of options, before stepping in with a solution.

The disciples' reaction when things got terribly bad, results in a miracle. It's worth paying attention to their next steps.

"The disciples woke him and said to him, 'Teacher, don't you care if we drown?'"

With a boat that handled like driftwood on a blown-out river in Spring, they wake Jesus. One of the disciples must have grabbed His shoulder, dripping all over Jesus while shaking Him awake. The words they use are powerful.

"Teacher…"

Someone shouts (I would guess Peter), "Teacher, wake up!" That's what Jesus was, a teacher (*didaskalos* in Greek). They were disciples. He was their teacher. The disciples were about to discover a new name for Jesus.

"…Don't you care?"

The unnamed speaker, talking for the entire group, no doubt asked a fundamental human question when facing a life-threatening situation; "Don't you care?" The questioning of Christ's love goes to the heart of the disciples fear, and to ours, as well. When life hits us with all of its ugliness, it can make us wonder, does God care? That question goes deep. Asking, "Don't you care?" comes from the soul. If God doesn't care, we reason, there is no hope. Ever. This question rarely surfaces when we scrape a knee or elbow. It gushes up like Old Faithful, with blasts of boiling steam, when the pressure of our life becomes greater than our faith. This question got Jesus' attention. It was a loaded question. Underneath it was, "If you care, you'd do something here. If you don't, we're all going to die." Jesus does something never seen before in recorded history: He quiets the storm. The Gospel of Mark says that,

"He got up, rebuked the wind and said to the waves, "Quiet! Be still!" Then the wind died down and it was completely calm."

Jesus was still lying on a cushion in the back of the boat when the disciples found Him. They brought Him up to speed on the danger they were facing and how the boat was falling apart and maybe implied that "Someone" wasn't doing His job. My human side, and the text, seems to indicate that Jesus might have been a little irritated. Who among us hasn't expressed our lack of appreciation when woken from a dead sleep?

Like a father who'd had enough from an unruly child, Jesus tells the angry storm to "Shut Up!" The Greek flavor of this text suggests that it happened immediately, instantly, right when he spoke it… BOOM…

everything went calm. There wasn't even the hint of a storm after Jesus spoke, or wind to fill a sail. According the Greek text, the seas became *megas* calm—mega calm, after being *megas* unruly.

Jesus answered their question, Do you care? With "Yes, I care." He spoke by deed. Not only did He show His compassion, He showed His power, His Mastery, His God-ness, like never before. It rocked their world to the core. The disciples didn't see this coming, either. Jesus, the Teacher, quieting the worst storm they may have ever experienced, *instantly*. Jewish boys had grown up hearing about the miracles of the ten plagues cast on Egypt, and a few others. Those were stories; this was astounding.

Jesus confronted this storm and calmed it. He wasn't done with this object lesson yet. Jesus responds to the disciples question with emotive questions of His own, questions of the heart. I believe that their words, doubting his love for them, *cut Him, as well.* The disciples had given up on faith and were giving in to their fears. They needed to be confronted, for they were going to face greater storms in the future. Jesus pushes back and asks,

"Why are you so afraid? Do you still have no faith?"

He didn't lecture. Jesus never demeaned anyone or made them feel worthless. Instead, He got to the heart of the matter: *fear and faith cannot co-exist in a person's soul.* To have faith is to trust the nature, the character, the essence of the person in question: Perfect Love. Crazy Love. His men still did not know Him. In a very clear way, Jesus was asking them: "Was my presence not enough?" There's an old saying that ties in with this; "You'll never know God is all you need, until you realize, God is all you have."

Jesus's question didn't quell the disciples' fears, however. Their fear amplified. Scripture says,

"They were terrified and asked each other, "Who is this? Even the wind and the waves obey him!""

Who wouldn't have been totally freaked out by a miracle like this? For the rest of their lives, they never forgot what happened that day, Who was in their midst. In the last line of this amazing narrative, lies a question, that we too, must never forget: "*Who is this?*" (Mark 4:41). Their asking tells us a lot about where the disciples were mentally in that moment. Their "God-box" was busted wide open. Jesus deconstructs their view of Him. Storms, whatever their source, will smash bad theology.

Each and every one of us has a "God-box", often made by our own minds. Maybe this box is sophisticated and we have labels on it like: Catholic, Orthodox, Evangelical, Arminian, Calvinist, and pre-Millennialist. We all have expectations of God and beliefs about Him. Some are actually biblical. Others feel biblical, but in the end, crumble like the idols they are and get torn down by the true Jesus. Who gave Jesus the most grief in his short three-year ministry? Religious people: Pharisees, Sadducees, and Zealots. These were people who knew Scripture, but who had never let the Author of Scripture take possession of them. Who were Christ's most devoted followers? "Sinners." People broken by the storms of life; people who had run out of options. People who had made a litany of bad choices landing them in bad places. People who had run out of options. They were a salty, gritty lot: whores, liars, drunks, and thieves. Yet, out of their brokenness, they found the One who gave them peace: Jesus. Jesus, who calmed their storm ravaged souls.

Bill's Story

Years ago, I took a phone call from a man that I barely knew. Let's call him Bill. I had borrowed a PA system from Bill to use in my startup church. Little did I know that this man was a raging alcoholic and drug addict. His wife knew. His friends knew. God knew. Bill's company discovered his addiction and cared enough to force him into treatment. Treatment was no small disruption. Bill later shared with me that on his first night in Valley Hope, a drug rehabilitation center, alone, hurting and reeling from his condition, he got down on his knees and prayed the sincerest prayer of his life. "Lord, help me." Three words. Nothing fancy. Just the cry of a broken heart and a wounded soul. In that moment, God heard Bill's cry for help, and made Himself real to him. God reached down, and calmed the storm that had been raging in Bill's heart for most of his life.

I'd like to say that from that day forward Bill never longed for another drop of alcohol or hit of cocaine. It wouldn't be true. Most addicts crave the object of their attention almost every day. Bill did take the necessary steps to change his life. He completed his inpatient treatment and attended 90 AA (Alcoholics Anonymous) meetings in 90 days. Bill worked a 12 Step program like his life depended on it. Bill started coming to church every week and joined a Bible study. Soon after, he was baptized, and experienced a spiritual resurrection (Acts 2:38; Rom. 6).

Several years later after Bill completed a local course of study that prepared him for ministry. I had the privilege of ordaining him soon after. While our paths eventually took us to different geographical regions, we've stayed in touch. More than 20 years have passed and my friend is still in love with Jesus, and he's still sober.

There isn't any disruptive storm in your life that God can't redeem for His glory and your ultimate good. In the case of the disciples, this storm-experience helped lay a foundation of faith in Christ that later became unshakeable. This story is simple. It is about giving up and asking for Jesus' help. History tells us that all the remaining 11 disciples, except the Apostle John, were later martyred, killed for their faith in Jesus. Martyrdom may sound romantic centuries later, but it was brutal.

Let us understand this one thing; the Apostles had such a faith in Jesus, that not even the threat of death made them recant. Storms can make us stronger with Jesus help.

Christ as Disrupter: Becoming His Disciple

God may have brought you to this book as a means to introduce you to Jesus. Maybe you were hurting and a friend gave it to you. Maybe you were browsing at a bookstore and found the title interesting and bought a copy. Maybe you spotted it at a garage sale for 50 cents and thought, "What do I have to lose?" and bought it. How you got this book is up to God. I believe that He put it into your life for a reason. That's why I wrote it. To help people make sense of the senseless things of this world.

So, I say to you, "Meet Jesus, the Disrupter." Both Paul and Peter refer to Jesus as a stumbling block (1 Cor. 1:23; 1 Pet. 2:8). What's a stumbling block? It a rock or masonry block that fell onto a road or path. It is so big, that you have to deal with its presence, by going around, over or under it. It's so big and laying such a way, that you might even trip over it. Thus, "a stumbling block." It's a storm in solid form!

Let me ask a life changing question; "What will you do with Jesus?" Regardless of what's going on in your life right now, be it positive or negative, you are right where you need to be, to meet Jesus. Remember, He's already in the boat with you. So what will you do? Will you keep bailing water until the ship sinks? Will you jump ship and hope you can swim to shore? Will you turn to Him in faith? (John 3:16). Will you become a disciple of Jesus? (Acts 2:38).

I wrote this book with a prayer that it would bring hope to those who follow Jesus and bring others into the Way (Acts 19:9). I encourage all my readers to get connected to Christ's church and experience the power of a faith community. In this Gospel story (Mark 4), there were a group of disciples experiencing disruption together. That's the way it should be. There is a bible believing church near you, small or large, where you can find a place to belong. I would encourage you to join the church. Get baptized. Take a class. Join a small group. Invite others onto the path. Follow Jesus through thick and thin for the rest of your life. I promise you, in this journey, you will have hard times as Jesus predicted (John 16:33). But, in the trials of life, you will meet God, make friends, experience personal growth, and bless the world.

Questions for Discussion

1. What topic or point jumped out of this chapter the most for you? Explain.

2. What part of the story, Jesus Quieting the Storm, do you relate to the most today? Explain.

3. What goes through your mind when you realize that you have One who can calm the seas and is also *IN* the boat with you during the storm?

4. How do you handle the times in your life when it feels like Jesus is sleeping? Explain.

5. Share a time when Christ did something special in your life.

6. How would you describe your relationship with Jesus today: Watching from a distance? Riding in the boat with Jesus? Willing to go wherever He leads? Explain.

7. What steps to you need to take to deepen your walk with Jesus?

About the Author

Dr. Tony L. Nelson

Tony earned a B.A. from Nebraska Christian College (1981), an M.A. in Practical Ministry from Cincinnati Christian College and Seminary (1990) and a Doctor of Ministry in Leadership and Spiritual Formation from George Fox Seminary (2013). He is an ordained minister in the Independent Christian Church (American Reformation Movement). Tony has over 30 years of pastoral ministry experience, mostly as Senior Pastor. In that role, he came along side hundreds of people who have experienced significant disruption and sought spiritual direction.

Tony most recently served a congregation numbering close to 1,000 members and attenders in a small resort town in North Idaho.

He is currently serving as a regional director for church planting in the Inland Northwest. He is recruiting, coaching and mentoring a whole new generation of dynamic church leaders. He has also launched Refuge-Idaho, an outdoors oriented pastor-care ministry utilizing a Guest Ranch.

Tony has served on multiple non-profit boards for various Christian organizations and institutions. He is a sought after leader, speaker and mentor. Tony is husband to Disa, who is a highly successful leader in her own right, currently a Mary Kay Independent Future Executive Senior Sales Director with over 30 years of experience.

Tony and Disa have two adult children, Craig and Carli (married to Adam) and one Yorkie named Rascal. Tony is an avid outdoorsman and can be found hunting, fishing, shooting, hiking, boating, or alpine skiing in scenic North Idaho, every chance he gets.

Appendix

Understanding Depression

What is depression? What forms does it take? Is depression ever healthy? These kinds of questions are good questions. Again, the purpose of this section is to not unpack everything there is to know about depression, but perhaps will offer a starting point for discovering and treating it.

Many good books have already written about depression and I'm sure more are on their way to print. A quick Internet search will turn up more books than you could read in a couple of years. Depression is real and can be life-threatening. If there is someone you know who is at risk, you can call the National Suicide Prevention Lifeline[19] They will guide you along a path to hopefully get that person some help.

Merriam-Webster simply states that depression is "a state of feeling sad; a serious medical condition in which a person feels very sad, hopeless, and unimportant and often is unable to live in a normal way."[20]

Defining something "simply", unfortunately doesn't equate to a simple treatment or cure. Depression can be a very complex and challenging experience to manage.

A couple of years ago couple my wife's depression seemed to be slowly getting worse. Disa was seeing a psychiatrist who kept prescribing different medications, which had very challenging side effects. So I decided, at my wife's request, to attend one of her appointments. It was very eye opening, to say the least. I began to question the doctor's treatment plan and kept asking about the long-term side effects of these medications. This doctor's standard answers to my queries were, "We can treat the side effects with additional medication." Pills to treat the pills. When I asked the doctor how often she actually reviewed my wife's chart there was a long pause as she glanced at the stack of client folders sitting on a small table next to her chair. I then pressed further and said, "You probably only looked at her chart five minutes before she came in here today, right?" She eluded the question, which in essence answered my question. This particular psychiatrist had a very large and growing practice so I understood her situation. However, I wanted someone who would treat my wife with more diligence.

Hear me: I'm *not* opposed to treating depression with medicine, but I am opposed to doing it blindly and without ongoing review. When I saw how chock-full the counter top was at home with my wife's meds, I decided to challenge her treatment plan. After discovering that the plan was primarily pharmaceutical and with little review—we decided to seek another direction.

My point is that sometimes a companion needs to step in and help those who suffer from major depression to get a better treatment plan because they can't always know what they need. In my opinion, my wife's psychiatrist wasn't trained to treat the root of her depression. Instead, she was just treating symptoms with pharmaceuticals. That's not to say pharmaceuticals aren't needed, because my wife still takes them. So, be the advocate! Hang in there, help your loved one get the treatment he or she needs. Leave no stone unturned.

Soon after our decision to seek other help for her depression, a Depression Recovery workshop[21] was offered at our local hospital. It was a video-based instructional program that included homework, and group discussion. Disa attended and found the program an extremely helpful part of her treatment plan. Much of the following material will stem from resources associated with this workshop, developed by Dr. Neil Nedley.

Depression—A Common Mental Illness

In his book, *Depression; the Way Out*, Dr. Nedley writes, "Depression is one of the most common, dangerous, and most feared forms of mental illness… All of us have times when we are 'down' or feel 'depressed.'"[22] He lists these facts about depression:

1. Major depression is the most common mood disorder.
2. It knows no cultural, social, or economic barriers.
3. It is largely misunderstood.
4. One out of three Internal Medicine patients has it.
5. Proper treatment can effectively reduce or cure it.
6. Most cases can be treated on an outpatient basis.

Types of Depression

Situational Depression

Situational depression is just what it sounds like—feelings of sadness resulting from some type of situation. "Depressive feelings will arise in the lives of all of us that result from traumatic events or other situations, but these are normal reactions that are not associated with a disease."[23] (e.g. Loss of a job, divorce, death of a loved one, disappointment in love and a "Blue Monday"). This is the kind of depression that I would describe as the "common cold" variety. Most of us know that feelings of depression associated with these kinds of situations will eventually ease up and disappear over time. This depression rarely requires medical intervention or a long-term counseling program. As a pastor, I'd say that the vast majority of people who seek counsel are suffering some form of *situational depression* and are usually receptive to some form of spiritual direction that alleviates it over a short period of time. Depression often serves a helpful purpose in one's healing after loss or traumatic experiences. Depression can make us slow down long enough to take a personal inventory of our lives. It can lead us to take time to sift through the "stuff" of life. Keeping those things that are important and tossing those that aren't. Everyone gets depressed. It is often a healthy response to our crazy lives.

Major or Chronic Depression

But what do we do when depressive feelings persist or become chronic? Dr. Nedley would suggest that a first step for someone struggling with a chronic form of depression is to get medical help. He labels this type of depression as a form of mental illness—a disease that can and should be treated medically and holistically (i.e. utilizing various combinations of exercise, diet and vitamin supplements). You may have just gotten hung up on the word, "disease," suggesting again how misunderstood chronic depression remains. Major depression is a form of mental illness. Period. To consider it any other way is to minimize its impact on the sufferer. This attitude would be akin to saying that skin cancer is nothing but a rash and should be treated with over-the-counter meds.

In an effort to help you do a little self-diagnosis I want to include Dr. Nedley's suggested symptoms for major depression. He suggests the following:

1. Deep sadness or emptiness.
2. Apathy.
3. Agitation or restlessness.
4. Sleep disturbances.
5. Weight/appetite disturbances.
6. Lack of concentration.
7. Feelings of excessive guilt or worthlessness.
8. Morbid thoughts.
9. Fatigue.

Nedley further explains that "a person who experiences at least five of the nine symptoms for at least two weeks has clinically defined *major depression*." And, "a person who experiences two to four of the nine symptoms for at least two weeks has a clinically defined mild form of depression." As I have already suggested, and Nedley emphasizes, all forms of major depression need to be treated. It is my observation, that in my small town there have been tragic deaths from suicide, especially of youths, that were probably caused by undiagnosed and untreated forms of major depression.

Nedley's work shows that the most successful treatment for major depression. Sometimes, leading to a cure, is a lifestyle treatment plan. As the name suggests, this treatment plan is no quick fix. It is a change in lifestyle. It is a change in the way depression is considered. Nedley's workshop suggests that a lifestyle plan includes an understanding of brain biology (how the brain works), healthy food choices (that impact the brain in positive ways) and nutritional supplements. Nedley claims that a significant number of those who successfully complete the workshop and apply the lifestyle treatment programs for up to 20 weeks see an improvement in their struggle with depression.

I am in complete agreement with Dr. Nedley who states, "Depression should not be tolerated as a lifelong condition with its miserable effects."[24]

What my wife and I really appreciated about Nedley's approach to major depression was his emphasis that the treatment for depression was holistic. His workshop taught that the alleviation of major depression— even possibly the cure—required addressing the emotional, physical and spiritual sides of life. Unlike many medical doctors or psychiatrists, who just prescribe a pill—only one facet of health—Dr. Nedley addresses a broader treatment plan.

BOOK II IN THE CRAZY BOOK SERIES
CRAZY LEADERSHIP
Uncovering Timeless Leadership Principles
that Bring Crazy Results
By Dr. Tony Nelson

Have you ever wondered how your heroes and heroines in life accomplish what they do? We are each given the same number of hours in a day; we all have inhibitions to overcome and storms to weather. "Regardless of what is in our bag of tricks: talents, smarts, finances, location," says Donna K. Wallace, "we are the sum of our days." We find strength and hope in another's story, and we find ourselves there, too. Your own story is being written each day. What legacy will you leave?

No one wants to be a mediocre leader. The crazy truth is that almost every household in America has a book of wisdom we can go to for wisdom immediately applicable as leaders. The Bible is full of incredible stories—crazy stories of leadership. How did God fashion a human resources plan and get Adam to embrace Eve? How did Noah survive the catastrophic flood with his family still intact? What was Abraham thinking when he took the senior citizens' tour of Israel? Nehemiah rebuilt the walls of Jerusalem in 100 days. Jonah ran from God and still changed an entire city. The Apostle Peter failed forward to become the pillar of Christ's Church.

The Apostle Paul a murderer-turned-author. Wherever you are in your leadership journey, you're sure to find camaraderie in the biblical characters and wisdom mined by Dr. Nelson.

In *Crazy Leadership,* Tony unpacks biblical characters within the paradigm of actionable leadership axioms, otherwise known as *self-evident truths.* The crazy thing about axioms is that we know them to be true, but until they are articulated as such, we miss their significance for our own application.

He will also weave in true stories of leaders from a variety of venues: direct sales, finance, non-profits, entrepreneurs, small business owners, and executives from larger companies. All will have a story to tell. Tony will focus on key truths and their applications to life and work.

At the end of each chapter will be discussion questions and other resources for further study. The book will not be focused on formulas for success, which really don't exist. Rather it will unpack principles and priorities that can be successfully translated into most leadership situations. A new and fresh look at these timeless leadership principles will certainly equip you for further personal growth that lead, to greater achievements.

Notes

1   Some of this material was taken from Jeremy Myers blog, "10 Christian Clichés to Avoid like the Plague," *Till He Comes* blog site (accessed 01-04-13).

2   Peterson, Eugene H., *THE MESSAGE: The Bible in contemporary Language*, NavPress, 2002.

3   http://www.forbes.com/companies/mary-kay (accessed 06-14-16).

4   http://www.forbes.com/companies/mary-kay (accessed 05-07-14).

5   Taken in part from the book, *Mary Kay Ash; Miracles Happen*.

6   In the late 1980's, I was at home one night when the phone rang. I picked it up and on the other end I heard, "Hi, this is Mary Kay, is Disa home? May I speak with her?" I said yes, and covered the phone with my hand and called to my wife, "Disa, it's Mary Kay…!" I handed over the phone to her and shamelessly eaves dropped. They talked for several minutes. When Disa hung up the

phone, she smiled knowing she was one of the fortunate women to personally speak with a woman who forever changed the landscape for women across America.

7   http://www.redcross.org/about-us/history/clara-barton (accessed 05-08-14).

8   http://www.icnchildren.net/world-orpans-choir-icn (accessed 05-08-14).

9   http://time.com/4343129/chibok-girl-second-rescued-boko-haram/ (accessed 07-07-16)

10 Wilson, Bill, Dr. Bob Smith, *The Big Book of Alcoholics Anonymous*, Renegade Press, 417.

11 Brueggemann, Walter, *An Introduction to the Old Testament*, Westminster John. Knox Press, p 302.

12 The seven appearances of God to Abram are given in the following passages: Gen 12:1-3, Gen 13:14-17, Gen 14: 18-20, Gen 15, Gen 17:1-21, Gen 18, Gen 22.

13 Dallas Willard, *The Divine Conspiracy: Rediscovering our Hidden Life in God* (New York: HarperCollins Publishers, 1998) 15.

14 http://www.merriam-webster.com/dictionary/nerve (accessed 02-05-16).

15 http://www.brainyquote.com/quotes/quotes/h/helenkelle101340.html (accessed 05-16-16).

16 https://www.blueletterBible.org/lang/lexicon/lexicon.cfm?Strongs=G4647&t=NIV (accessed 06-02-16).

17 Dr. Dan Brunner.

18 Emphasis mine.

19 http://www.suicidepreventionlifeline.org/

20 http://www.merriam-webster.com/dictionary/depression (accessed 07-03-15).

21 See: http://nedleyhealthsolutions.com/index.php/programs/community-depression-recovery.html (accessed 07-03-15).

22 Neil Nedley, *Depression: The Way Out* (Ardmore, OK: Nedley Publishing, 2011), 6.

23 Ibid., 8.

24 Ibid., 232.

A free eBook edition is available with the purchase of this book.

To claim your free eBook edition:

1. Download the Shelfie app.
2. Write your name in upper case in the box.
3. Use the Shelfie app to submit a photo.
4. Download your eBook to any device.

Shelfie

A free eBook edition is available
with the purchase of this print book.

CLEARLY PRINT YOUR NAME ABOVE IN UPPER CASE

Instructions to claim your free eBook edition:
1. Download the Shelfie app for Android or iOS
2. Write your name in **UPPER CASE** above
3. Use the Shelfie app to submit a photo
4. Download your eBook to any device

Print & Digital Together Forever.

Snap a photo

Free eBook

Read anywhere

The Morgan James
Speakers Group

We connect Morgan James published authors with live and online events and audiences whom will benefit from their expertise.